TAP into Your Potential

TAP into Your Potential

How to Think, Act, and Practice Like an Entrepreneur

Rick De La Guardia

BEP

BUSINESS EXPERT PRESS

Leader in applied, concise business books

TAP into Your Potential: How to Think, Act, and Practice like an Entrepreneur

Copyright © Business Expert Press, LLC, 2020.

Cover design by Charlene Kronstedt

Interior design by Exeter Premedia Services Private Ltd., Chennai, India

First published in 2020 by
Business Expert Press, LLC
222 East 46th Street, New York, NY 10017
www.businessexpertpress.com

ISBN-13: 978-1-95253-886-5 (paperback)
ISBN-13: 978-1-95253-887-2 (e-book)

Business Expert Press Entrepreneurship and Small Business Management Collection

Collection ISSN: 1946-5653 (print)
Collection ISSN: 1946-5661 (electronic)

First edition: 2020

10 9 8 7 6 5 4 3 2 1

Abstract

There are many nuts and bolts and theoretical books on entrepreneurship available in the market today, but it is not the nuts and bolts nor theory that makes a true entrepreneur, it is adherence to the unique mindset and philosophy. This book focuses on the concepts, mindset, philosophy, and qualities of entrepreneurship and will provide guidance and suggest helpful activities at the end of each chapter to inspire the reader to take positive steps toward entrepreneurship. It will teach the reader how to Think, Act, and Practice like an entrepreneur.

Many of the author's personal experiences have been included throughout the book as real life examples of issues and decisions that the reader may face in their path toward entrepreneurship and to demonstrate that anyone can be an entrepreneur if they know what it takes and are shown how to go about it.

This book was designed to be read and be helpful to individuals of any age with entrepreneurial aspirations in any profession. In Chapter 8, this book contains a summary of helpful advice, drawn out by the author, from successful entrepreneurs working in specialties across a spectrum of 12 different professions. This will provide the reader a broad understanding of what it takes to be successful in a variety of fields. Chapter 8 also contains a piece written from an often-forgotten perspective, that of the significant other. This will provide the reader an understanding of some of the sacrifices required as well as the potential rewards for those closest to them.

The premise of this book is on the entrepreneurial way of life and it will focus on the three key concepts as follows:

1. Part I: How to Think Like an Entrepreneurship.
2. Part II: How to Act Like an Entrepreneur.
3. Part III: How to Practice Like an Entrepreneur.

This book will outline the *Seven Key Qualities That Are Integral To Successful Entrepreneurship*, identify the *Six Main Concepts Of The Entrepreneurial Mindset* and detail how and what entrepreneurs think about. It will offer a new and alternative definition of what a true entrepreneur is and how it differs from the conventional definition. It will expose the *Seven Key Differences Between Being An Entrepreneur Versus Just Being A Business Owner*. It will touch on how to focus on investing and not on over-consuming. It will detail the differences between assets and liabilities, explain how to buy your homes wisely, and teach you how to manage, maximize, and grow your 401(k) to put you in position to fund your startup. It will help you define what success means to you so that you can set goals and identify paths to attain them. It will encourage you to emulate the best and help you identify areas of specialty in which you can provide a product or service faster, better, or "cheaper" than anyone else to help maximize success. It will identify the *Five Steps To Achieve Success*. It will discuss how to prepare your business to adapt and survive during difficult economic times. Finally, it will teach you how to create credentials, master self-promotion, seek recognition, network, and originate business.

Being an entrepreneur is not easy and it can, and will, be difficult at times but it can also be extremely rewarding and liberating. The saying "if I can do it…you can do it too" holds true. The book will not only show you how to do it, but it will also provide firsthand accounts and personal experiences and details of how I did it, including the hurdles I encountered and how I overcame them. The personal information and experiences provided in this book are not intended to be a success story as it also contains examples of failures along the way. It is instead a story of personal perseverance, determination, overcoming obstacles and is still very much a work in progress. It is written with the intent of providing the reader a road map of how I did it and how you can do it better.

They say hindsight is 20/20 and they are right. I am only in the position to advise the reader because of my experiences, successes and even the mistakes made on my personal path to entrepreneurship. It is much easier for me to tell you what to do, since I have already gone through it myself. I know what worked and did not work for me. I remember the mistakes I made and the successes I had. Now, I wish to share those with you in the hopes that it makes your path toward entrepreneurship easier, and your successes greater, than mine. Remember that regardless of what you get out of this book, it is ultimately up to you to put what you learn into practice to begin to realize your dream of entrepreneurship.

Keywords

entrepreneur; business; success; invest; goal; think; mind; professional; potential; career

Contents

Foreword

When one keeps hearing someone's name in various circles, one begins to think this is a person to meet. Such is the case with Rick De La Guardia. Through my dealings as the director of the Entrepreneurship Program at the University of Miami Herbert Business School, at any given entrepreneurship networking event, I would hear his name. Time and time again, people would ask me if I had met Rick and would extol his virtues as an advocate for young entrepreneurs. His reputation preceded him. Before long, Rick and I got to collaborate on work connecting engineering and business students to foster entrepreneurship and innovation.

Since that first endeavor, over the years, I have had the distinct honor of volunteering alongside Rick, empowering young people to challenge themselves and following their entrepreneurial dreams. Rick is a dedicated and passionate individual, making time to mentor students, hear their start-up pitches, and provide candid and invaluable advice. His approach is always one that challenges and yet empowers. Every person I know who has had the pleasure of receiving Rick's coaching has walked away a stronger person, with a better grasp of what to expect and how to go after their goals.

My students have instantly felt a connection to Rick, through his unique ability to read these young entrepreneurs and get to the core of their needs. Rick not only has the technical know-how, the command of financials, and understanding of the needs of the business, he possesses unbelievable emotional intelligence. Working with young people just making their way could actually be his calling. He has mentored my students, one-on-one, taking time to offer a tailored approach to each young entrepreneur. He takes great care to not only thoroughly analyze the challenges they face; he makes sure to wrap that in a personal coaching session that builds them up and prepares them mentally for the challenges they will face.

In Rick's first book, *Engineer to Entrepreneur*, he took the engineer and created a paradigm shift to prepare them for entrepreneurship. It is a perfect transition, as in many cases, the engineer is the inventor and innovator, but not necessarily the businessperson. His first book is an easy guide to preparing the engineer not only technically, but also mentally to enter the complicated world of entrepreneurship. I highly recommend it.

This book, much like his first, is an easy guide for anyone who is considering becoming an entrepreneur. Rick's analytical and logical mind has created an easy, step-by-step playbook, complete with exercises to enable anyone to reach their goal of becoming a successful entrepreneur. I see a lot of what he has done in person with my students in this book. He has refined his practice of encouragement and empowerment and distilled it into this step-by-step guide to help anyone get started, stay focused, stay on track, persevere despite any setbacks, and ultimately, succeed.

Entrepreneurship can be treacherous and unpredictable, but this book is honest, sets realistic expectations of the path you are about to traverse, and offers you support along the way. My students should all graduate with a copy of this book tucked under their arm. Follow this guide and you will be well on your way to being an entrepreneur.

Susy Alvarez-Diaz, MBA
Senior Lecturer, Miami Herbert Business School
University of Miami
CEO, ADG Omnimedia
Miami, Florida

Susy Alvarez-Díaz is a senior lecturer teaching undergraduate entrepreneurship courses through the Department of Management at the University of Miami Herbert Business School, and graduate entrepreneurship courses in the MVSIO program at Bascom Palmer Eye Institute. She has been teaching at the college level over the last 16 years. She is the former director of Entrepreneurship Programs at the University of Miami where she more than doubled enrollment, tripled the participation in the annual Business Plan Competition, and hosted ABC's Shark Tank two years in a row, the only university in all of Florida to do so.

Mrs. Alvarez-Diaz graduated with honors from the University of Miami with a Bachelor of Business Administration degree in International Finance and Marketing. She then went on to complete a Master of Business Administration degree in Marketing and Management. She is currently pursuing a doctorate in Higher Education and Leadership at the University of Miami.

She has almost 30 years' experience in marketing and corporate communications, including public relations, branding, internal communications, public affairs, and community and university relations. As an entrepreneur for the last 18 years, she is CEO of ADG Omnimedia—a public relations and marketing firm in Miami, Florida. She served as a coach for Babson College's inaugural class of WIN Lab in Miami and a mentor at Miami Dade College's Idea Center. Alvarez-Diaz is regularly featured in national media outlets such as *CNN Español* and was presented with the *Excellence in Teaching* award from the Miami Herbert Business School in 2018. Currently, she is the faculty advisor for Women in Business and uStart Entrepreneurship Club.

Previously, Alvarez-Diaz worked for Hewlett-Packard's Latin America region, launching marketing campaigns and promotions with sales distributors. As the Latin America Region Communications and Public Relations Manager, she then worked on the successful and historic IPO of HP's spin-off, Agilent Technologies, Inc. She also served as the media and PR consultant to the President and CEO during his VIP visits to the region.

Preface

My father's influence on me was strong, and it instilled in me a tremendous sense of work ethic and ambition. He showed me, by example, how to work hard, never give up, and chase your dreams. Discipline was high on his list of priorities as a father. He was a man of few words. He rarely told me how to do things, but rather showed me how. I grew up, along with my older brother, in an environment that today would be frowned upon as a method or form to raise your children. My father would not accept failure, quitting, or complaining of any sort from us. He demanded unquestioned obedience and perfection. If we failed, quit, or complained, he would make his displeasure immediately and well known to the point that we would not dare repeat the same infraction, whatever that infraction was at that day and time. He gave us a lot of responsibility, at a young age; sometimes, I felt it was too much. His influence over us and his strict form of discipline and control did not emanate from a sense of dominance or from a dark place, of that I am certain. He loved us very much, of that too, I am sure. It came, I feel, from a sense of duty and responsibility. It was his job to teach us and prepare us to be men in a very tough world. He had come from a similar upbringing, much worse than what he imposed on us, or so I am told. He was strict, but fair. I can say that only in hindsight. I do not dare ask the 15-year-old version of myself that same question for fear of a vastly different answer. My eyes swell and tears form around them as I write this and begin to recall my relationship with my father. But not because of the hardship, not because of the punishments, not because of the hard work or sacrifices he imposed upon us. You see, I was a stubborn young man, much like him I am told, and I could, and did, take anything he threw my way. No, the tears form because I miss him so much. He died without giving me a chance to say goodbye, without giving me a chance to get to know him. You see, I never *knew* my dad. I spent most of my childhood mad at him. We rarely talked about anything, except work. I was mad at him for making me miss out on my childhood. I was mad at him for a countess number of reasons.

My father and I never really had an open relationship. Based on that lack of personal foundation, as a young man, I did not know how to talk to him or what to talk to him about. All our communications were short and to the point. Eventually, we stopped talking all together. As I grew older, he lost control over me due to a tragic incident where he was shot and paralyzed. An incident that I partly blame on myself. In my mind, if I had done what I was taught and told to do, and if I had been ever vigilant and warned him of the oncoming danger, perhaps there may have been a different outcome to that night. A night that changed his life forever.

Not too long after, I then lost control over myself. I did not know what to do with my newfound freedom. Because of that, I struggled early on at the university. The benefits of being gifted with so much responsibility early on in life is valuable experience. The cost of being burdened with so much responsibility so young in life is the sacrifice of youthful whims and folly. I started paying my dues early in life. Do I regret it? His strict and formal way of teaching? I still struggle answering that question to this day. Am I better off for it, as a professional? Absolutely. Am I better off for it, as a person? That is a harder question to answer, and I would not be the right person to ask. I had to learn that part, the social part, the soft skills, later in life. Life tossed me around a bit, early on, socially, and academically before I learned to right the ship. If it not for a very understanding and caring university official, I would not be on my second book on inspiring people to never give up and always follow their dreams. You see, I had help along the way.

The steering currents of life are ever-changing; you must be ever vigilant and improvise, adapt, and overcome or risk being swept away, drifting aimlessly in your life or in your career. You must take control of your life, both in the professional and the social aspects. Do not let life take control away from you. It will if you let it. There are many other good books out there to teach you how to take control of your social life. This book will teach you how to take control of your professional life, by following the path of entrepreneurship.

As I got older, and closer to entrepreneurship, I learned a lot from some colleagues on how to carry on as a professional, especially from my late, former, boss at my first engineering job and from a very tough city building official. Both showed me the importance of being well rounded, versatile, meticulous, to pay attention to detail, and to be honest and dependable.

Early on in life, I found very few resources on how to manage my career until I happened upon a book titled *Rich Dad, Poor Dad* by Robert Kiyosaki. That book inspired me and introduced me to the concept of entrepreneurship. It taught me to think outside the box and break away from the social conventions of play it safe, do not rock the boat, save your money, put in your time, and do not take any risks. I would go on to write my own book to try and inspire others to follow the entrepreneurial path titled *Engineer to Entrepreneur: Success Strategies to Manage Your Career and Start Your Own Firm* (e2E), published by the American Society of Civil Engineers. That book was geared more to help those in my chosen profession of engineering, and because of its success, and after many requests from nonengineering students and professionals, I decided to write this book and make it applicable to all careers and disciplines. Whereas my first book is more technical and practical, it teaches you the actual steps to plan for, and start, your own company, this book is more motivational and touches on the concept of entrepreneurship and the mindset and tools needed. In chapters 10 and 11, I reference and use excerpts from my first book (e2E) to provide the reader a source of additional information. *"Excerpts from Engineer to Entrepreneur © 2016 American Society of Civil Engineers used with permission of the publisher. All rights reserved."*

My fathers' influence on me is forever engrained in my sense of hard work and determination. His influence not only provided lessons on what to do, but it also provided examples and taught me what not to do. It gave me a sense of wanting to find ways to accomplish the same goals differently and finding the right balance in life. The inspiration for this book comes, as a tribute to him, and, as a sense of duty and responsibility. It is my attempt to teach and prepare you, to the best of my ability, to be successful entrepreneurs in a very tough world. You all have it inside of you if you just learn to TAP into your potential. Think like an entrepreneur, act like an entrepreneur, and practice like an entrepreneur.

Acknowledgments

Book reviewers: I want to thank the individuals who volunteered to read an advanced copy of the manuscript and provide valuable feedback. *Mario Avalos, Jaime Mitrani, Anna Cook, and Lina Sekkat.*

Book contributors: I want to thank all of the successful entrepreneurs who contributed to the book by allowing me to draw out and tell their stories for the benefit of the readers: *Flor Mayoral* (medicine), *Anthony Lopez* (law), *Anthony Fasano* (engineering), *Daphne Gurri* (architecture), *Philip Shechter* (accounting), *Jaime Mitrani* (business), *James Tate* (construction), *George Haj* (media relations), *Mario Avalos* (real estate), *Walter Aleman* (photography), *Juan Carlos Bermudez* (politics), *Ana VeigaMilton* (philanthropy), and *Frances G. De La Guardia* (the significant other).

Alvaro Diaz-Rubio: I want to thank Alvaro for his great talent and patience in creating the original illustrations used in the book. You can see his work at the beginning of Parts 1, 2, and 3 of the book.

Susana (Susy) Alvarez-Diaz: I want to thank Susy for agreeing to write the foreword for the book and for trusting me to judge and mentor so many of her students' business pitches. I enjoyed all the interactions with her and her students.

Michael Phang, PhD, P.E.: Thank you, posthumously, for believing in me, for understanding my situation, and giving me a second chance at life. I am forever grateful to have met you and learn from you both in the classroom and in life. It was a true honor when your equally talented and successful daughter, Katie, invoked my recollection to her of how you handled my academic case, when I was a university student who was lost and in need of help, as an example of your influence and kindness to all who came to see you off. You would have been so proud of her. Rest in peace knowing that you have made an indelible and positive difference in so many people's lives during your time here on earth. That is the truest measure of a person. I am not the only person who can attest to that, of that I am sure, but I am ever grateful to you, that I can so attest. To Katie, I hope you take some solace in knowing how much he did for so many people.

Humayoun Farooq, PhD, P.E. and Peter Iglesias, P.E.: Both individuals, whether they knew or know it or not, were very influential in my eventual path to engineering and entrepreneurship. Both were mentors. One was a strict boss; the other a strict building official. Thank you both for the learning opportunities and confidence you showed in me as a young engineer and eventual entrepreneur.

Frances G. De La Guardia: My wife Frances, a very successful professional in her own right, was instrumental in not only nudging me to follow my dream of opening my own firm, but was an avid supporter of and investor in the company. She has made countless sacrifices along the way, without which I would not have been able to realize my dream. I am forever grateful for her love and support. You will learn more about her in Chapter 8.

Carmen L. De La Guardia and Rodolfo H. De La Guardia: I am who I am today because of my mother and father. Carmen Leysis De La Guardia and Rodolfo Humberto De La Guardia. My mother provided most of the love and nurturing for our family and still does to this day. She is the perfect example of sacrifice in the name of, and for the benefit of, her children. My father instilled most of the discipline and taught us the necessary life skills. I am the second child of four. I have an older brother, *Rodolfo Humberto De La Guardia, Jr.*, and two younger siblings, *Gustavo Adolfo De La Guardia* and *Ana Matilde De La Guardia-Paiz*. My mother has made, and continues to make, untold sacrifices to make sure her children are well taken care of. I am eternally grateful to her for that.

When it comes to my professional career, that, I owe all to my father. I honestly feel, despite all the hard times we went through growing up, that I would not be successful today if it were not for the lessons he taught me. You see, my father was a strict man, but he was also a smart, hardworking man. He was shot and paralyzed in the 1980s while working a typical late night at a gas station he owned, next to a business he had setup, after a full workday at his day job. He did all of this to put all his four children through private school and college. There are people in this world who say they love you and then there are people in this world who show you they love you. My father was the latter. My father died in 2009 from complications after his assault, and I never got to say goodbye or thank him for all his sacrifices. I grew up with an internal resentment due to his strict form of discipline, and I never learned to cope with it. I never understood him. Even as he was dying, he maintained his stubborn beliefs and did not reach out, or let others reach out, and let me know of his condition. He felt that if I were told of his situation, that I would feel pity and reach out solely for that reason. He was wrong in thinking that; I was wrong in not reaching out more. But, he died thinking I did not care about him. *Dad, I do love you, very much and I miss you.* Thank you for all your sacrifices, for all your hard work, and for the examples you taught us. *I dedicate this book to you. Te quiero mucho!*

Introduction

Before we get started…I believe it is particularly important, when getting advice from someone, to know and understand where that person is coming from and how they arrived at their perspective. My father's influence and my upbringing were the main reasons I decided to become an engineer and ultimately an entrepreneur. My father was a combination, mechanic, electrician, handyman, engineer, entrepreneur, and overall problem solver. He owned a gas station and a mechanic and parts shop where my older brother and I spent most of our free time working during our youth. Working at the gas station and mechanic shop exposed me to many learning opportunities at a young age. Since before and throughout high school, I was learning and doing many tasks that people would normally pay a professional to do. That work included working with cars, masonry, carpentry, electricity, and plumbing. I also worked on building and installing custom security bars, building reinforced masonry walls, laying, and installing chained link fences and dismantling cars, bought at auction, for useable parts.

In addition to the aforementioned, I also worked at the gas station pumping gas, fixing flats, changing oil, installing tires, and repairing cars. My brother and I would also be responsible for doing all the house chores, including yard work, repairs, and cleaning. In the process of completing all these responsibilities and chores, I learned how to use almost every type of mechanical and power tool and how to solve problems. It was not an easy or typical childhood by any means, but it certainly taught me how to be resourceful, independent, and versatile. Not only was I able to take care of my own problems as a child, I was also able to resolve other people's problems.

My childhood upbringing and experiences helped hone my analytical skills. I spent a great deal of my childhood taking things apart and putting them back together, creating and building. To this day, I rarely hire a professional to fix a problem around the office or house, still preferring to do it myself. I like a challenge, and I love solving problems.

My first experience and exposure to entrepreneurship, aside from the examples I gathered from my father as I grew up, started when I responded to an ad in the halls of the college of engineering at the University of Miami for a part-time position in an engineering office. Even though the position I applied for entailed only clerical work, initially, it did provide me with my very first exposure to the importance of having a specialty within the engineering field. I started working as a file clerk, typing, running plans, and making blueprints. Soon after, I was assigned bookkeeping and office management responsibilities. I handled the setup of the office medical and retirement plans. Thereafter, my responsibilities increased to encompass office accounting (quarterly reports, profit, and loss statements), including learning the software. I would go on to upgrade the general office software and prepare more efficient calculation templates using Excel and eventually learned and implemented the QuickBooks accounting software and processed payroll. I was also writing all the project job proposals, testing proposals, and inspection reports.

Then, my first chance at engineering presented itself when I suggested transitioning the drawings produced at the office from hand drafting to computer drafting. I had taken and exceled in my computer-aided design and drafting (CADD) class in school and was given the opportunity. I took advantage of the challenge, and it paid off. Quickly thereafter, I helped complete the transition by installing and configuring the software and new plotter, including creating the new drawing templates. I was so successful in convincing the firm of the benefits of computer drafting that the company decided to hire a full-time AutoCAD operator, as I was part time and the workload had grown too much for me to handle alone.

Once I was no longer solely responsible for the drafting, I began learning to review plans and perform inspections under the supervision of another staff member. I was quickly given more and more inspection responsibilities, and I exceled at that as well. Then, after graduation, I was offered a full-time position as an engineer with the firm. The pay was not optimal, and I kept getting nontechnical projects to work on; however, I was told, by my boss, that one day, those nontechnical skills would be valuable. He was right.

I eventually held every possible position that could be offered at an engineering firm (clerk, bookkeeper, draftsman, office manager, accountant, inspector, engineer, human resources, and project manager). That job lasted 13 years and is the main reason that today I own my own engineering firm. I consider my time there as valuable learning experience of how to run and manage an engineering company.

I have only had three engineering jobs in my professional career, the aforementioned part-time job that turned into a 13-year apprenticeship, a three-year stint at a general structural engineering firm, in which I established and implemented my field of specialty and oversaw its development, and my current venture going on 10 years of owning my own engineering firm. Between those three jobs, based on the tasks I was asked to perform, I managed to accumulate the equivalent of approximately 26 years of experience in overseeing engineering office operations.

It was not until I became a business owner that I started to piece together all the concepts of true entrepreneurship and learned to distinguish the difference between being just a business owner and an entrepreneur. I took the lessons learned from reading the book *Rich Dad, Poor Dad* and I started to apply them. Along the way, I developed my own opinions based on my own experiences, and in 2014, I started to write my own book on entrepreneurship to try and pay it forward.

My first book, *Engineer to Entrepreneur: Success Strategies to Manage Your Career and Start You Own Firm* (e2E) was published in 2016 by the American Society of Civil Engineers. By the time of the publication, I had come to fully understand what an entrepreneur truly is. I had made sacrifices, taken risks, planned, invested, created, and grown my brand, published my work and mentored many students and young engineers. In chapters 10 and 11, I reference and use excerpts from that book (e2E) to provide the reader a source of additional information. *"Excerpts from Engineer to Entrepreneur © 2016 American Society of Civil Engineers used with permission of the publisher. All rights reserved."* That book was so well received by the engineering community that word started getting out to students with interest in other professions. I started judging business plan pitches at the Herbert School of Business at the University of Miami and getting requests from people in all professions to share my experiences with them and write a book applicable to all. That is how this book, which I call TAP, for short, was conceived. Now, let us get started…

PART I

How to Think Like an Entrepreneur

This part of the book will focus on how to think like an entrepreneur. But, before you learn how to think like an entrepreneur, you need to learn and understand: What is an entrepreneur? What do entrepreneurs think about? What is the entrepreneurial mindset? These are the questions that I will answer in the first part of this book. To understand what an entrepreneur is, first, you need to identify and study their common key qualities. Once you become aware of the key qualities of an entrepreneur, and you learn how they think and what they think about, and understand their specific way of looking at the world, then you will have a good map and blueprint for your future and for success. Success and opportunities are out there for everyone, if they have a good map and blueprint to follow, as well as the desire and determination to chase their dreams until they succeed.

In Chapter 1, I will discuss why I believe that the most common definition of what an entrepreneur is, is wrong. I will explain why and offer up my own definition of what an entrepreneur is. I will make the distinction between being an entrepreneur versus being just a business owner. You can own a business and not be an entrepreneur, and you can be an entrepreneur without owning a business.

In Chapter 2, I will teach you how to think, and I will explain how entrepreneurs think differently than most people. I will explain how they come up with their ideas, as well as where those ideas come from. There are many theories on where ideas come from. Some people believe that ideas come from an accumulation of life experiences, stored memories, a collective subconscious, through dreams, via meditation, or even prayers. I will provide my own thoughts on the subject. After I explain how to think, I will teach you how to think like an entrepreneur and what entrepreneurs think about. Thinking, and grasping ideas, is the key to a successful future in entrepreneurship. Thinking is more of an art form than a process. A misunderstood art form, in my opinion. It is a simple concept that most people have forgotten. Learning how to think and how to tap into ideas is easier than you might believe, if you have a map, but it requires strong resolve and discipline to learn how to think. Done properly, it can lead to a wealth of riches at the end. Consider it like following a map and finding a hidden treasure of which only you know the location and tapping into it whenever the need arises. But, instead of material wealth, you would be tapping into a hidden source of knowledge that only you can reach if you just open your mind. Ideas are born of thinking, and without good ideas, there is no path to success.

In Chapter 3, I will explain how being an entrepreneur is a way of life and requires a specific mindset. I will explain what that mindset is and introduce the six main concepts of the entrepreneurial mindset. Concepts that I believe are so important that I have dedicated a large portion of the book to explaining why I believe they are so critical to entrepreneurship and how it distinguishes an individual from just being a business owner versus being an entrepreneur. Entrepreneurship is a way of life. My first, and most influential exposure, aside from the lessons I learned from my father, and the experiences gained as a young engineer, to this way of life, came when I read the book *Rich Dad Poor Dad* by Robert Kiyosaki. For me, it was a career and mind-altering revelation. It literally changed my way of thinking and looking at my future with respect to my professional career. I went on to apply many of the concepts I learned in that book to my professional career. I also read how Robert Kiyosaki was himself inspired by reading *Think and Grow Rich* by Napoleon Hill. I found that book enlightening as well. I recommend you read both. I hope that by reading this book, I can affect the reader, you, in a similar way.

CHAPTER 1

What Is an Entrepreneur?

Being an entrepreneur is a way of life, a lifetime commitment to free yourself from the limits imposed on you by others and a conscious choice and desire to set your own path in life, limited only by your own ambitions.

This chapter will focus on the concept of a true entrepreneur, and it will answer the question of: What is an entrepreneur? Obviously, an entrepreneur is a person who practices entrepreneurship. But, the answer is not that simple. First, you need to identify what the current, or most accepted, definition of entrepreneurship is. Entrepreneurship has traditionally been defined as the process of designing, launching, and running a new business, or one that organizes, manages, and assumes the risks of a business or enterprise. This definition, in my opinion, does not truly portray what entrepreneurship is nor what true entrepreneurs endure on their paths to success. It also does not distinguish between a true entrepreneur versus just being a business owner nor does it expose the subtle and not-so-subtle differences between them.

True entrepreneurship goes far beyond that traditional definition and instead consists of seven key qualities that are integral to successful entrepreneurship. Those seven key qualities that must be demonstrated to call oneself a true entrepreneur are listed as follows:

The seven key qualities of entrepreneurship	
1	Avid investor
2	Idea seeker
3	Persistent action taker
4	Risk taker
5	Meticulous planner
6	Faithful practitioner
7	Credentials creator

Not coincidentally, based on the aforementioned, a much more accurate and purposeful definition of what entrepreneurship entails is:

Entrepreneurship is a *mindset* focused on *thoughts* and persistent *actions* without avoidance of *risk* involving the formulation of a *plan*, which is put to *practice*, in the creation and cultivation of a *brand*.

The Entrepreneurship Formula

If you want to become an entrepreneur, you need to study the seven key qualities of entrepreneurship and incorporate them into your way of life.

We will discuss the entrepreneurial mindset in detail in Chapter 3. For now, however, let us discuss in more detail the seven key qualities of a true entrepreneur.

1. *Avid Investor*: Focuses on finding and taking advantage of growth potential. Both financially and personally to increase worth in both areas. *Mindset.*

2. *Idea Seeker*: Focuses on problems that exist in society and ways to address them to make the world and their environment a better place. *Thoughts.*

3. *Persistent Action Taker*: Focuses on doing, and not just thinking, in the proactive and persistent pursuit of their goals. *Actions.*

4. *Risk Taker*: Focuses on the rewards associated with taking advantage of opportunities that present themselves, despite the risks. *Risk.*

5. *Meticulous Planner:* Focuses on creating a plan and outline for success that would allow themselves to mitigate risk and failure. *Plan*

6. *Faithful Practitioner:* Focuses on the implementation of their ideas for beneficial and practical use. *Practice*

7. *Credentials Creator:* Focuses on the creation and cultivation of a brand that will lead to name recognition and credibility. *Brand*

Owning and managing a business, in and of itself, does not earn someone the right to be considered an entrepreneur nor does the mere fact that a person starts, inherits, or purchases a business. You cannot just buy or inherit that title. For a business owner to earn the right to be considered an entrepreneur, they must mix in those seven key qualities into their business formula. Before I explain the differences between just being a business owner and an entrepreneur, I want to clarify that there is nothing wrong with just being a business owner. That is a tall task, in and of itself, and one to be celebrated and be extremely proud of. My following descriptions are generalized and not true of all people who are just business owners. They are only intended to show how entrepreneurs take business ownership to a different level. With that being said, the seven key differences between just being a business owner and being an entrepreneur are as follows:

1. *An entrepreneur has a certain mindset and lives their life according to a different set of rules with different goals involving much sacrifice and risk. They guide themselves by much more than financial success.* A person who is just a business owner is a person who may be in it primarily for the money and not willing or strong enough to make the needed sacrifices to take their business to the next level. They may not take the time to teach or give back to the community. They may use their revenue stream to enhance their stature with material goods and accumulate liabilities and not assets.

2. *An entrepreneur is relentless and always thinking and innovating and coming up with new ideas.* A person who is just a business owner is a person who may not think beyond the daily aspects of their company. They may be satisfied by just getting by and may not strive to be creative or innovative.

3. *An entrepreneur is proactive and persistently acts on their thoughts and ideas despite the fear of failure.* A person who is just a business owner is a person who may have great ideas, but may be too busy, scared, or simply does not know how to act on them.

4. *An entrepreneur does not succumb to the powerful deterrent to progress and success, that is, risk and the unknown. They learn to mitigate the risk and move forward with their ideas.* A person who is just a business owner is a person who may let the fear of failure control their actions or lack thereof.

5. *An entrepreneur plans meticulously to ensure success and takes control of their future.* A person who is just a business owner is a person who may go with the flow and lets life control them and their direction, paving the way for potential failure.

6. *An entrepreneur puts their plans and ideas to practice.* A person who is just a business owner is a person who may not plan nor create, implement, nor follow a plan.

7. *An entrepreneur creates credentials for themselves that set them apart from their peers and cultivates their brand.* A person who is just a business owner is a person who may not know that they are the brand and may not seek to continue learning and bettering themselves.

I have often paraphrased a saying that an entrepreneur is someone willing to do things for a part of their lives that most people will not, in order to be able to do things for the rest of their lives, that most people cannot. This is a catchy and overly simplistic definition, but, nonetheless, accurate.

Entrepreneurs have always been thought of as a different breed. Look back at history and you will see that the most successful entrepreneurs exemplified these qualities. *They had an idea, formulated a plan, invested in it, risked much to implement it, persistently acted to make it a reality, put it to practical use, and made a name for themselves.*

In summary and to answer the question of: What is an entrepreneur? *An entrepreneur is and individual who adopts a unique mindset constantly reinforced by thoughts and persistent actions without avoidance of risk and formulates a plan, which they put to practice, in the creation and cultivation of a brand.*

Chapter 1: What Is an Entrepreneur?

Recommended Activities

1. Study carefully the seven key qualities of entrepreneurship and see how you can begin to incorporate them into your daily lives.
2. Identify areas in your field in which you can obtain specialized skills or credentials.
3. Look up contemporary entrepreneurs in your respective field that you admire and reach out and connect with them on professional networking sites such as LinkedIn.
4. Make a list of successful alumni from your alma mater that you would like to model your career after and emulate and reach out to them for advice.
5. Research the great minds and entrepreneurs in history and identify what made them unique and successful. List qualities they have in common.

CHAPTER 2

What Do Entrepreneurs Think About?

Most of us have lost the true art of thinking. We, too often, allow our minds to be consumed and cluttered by mundane thoughts. We must train our minds to tune in and tap into the universal subconscious.

This chapter will focus on the mind of an entrepreneur and answer the question of: What do entrepreneurs think about? But, before you learn about what entrepreneurs think about, you need to learn how they think and how to think. In this age of overstimulation, we have lost the art of, desire, or quite frankly, the time to sit down and think.

Because it is impossible to separate thoughts and ideas from entrepreneurship and success, I find it imperative to discuss how ideas are formed and where they come from. It has been documented that many of history's brilliant minds, when asked how they came up with their ideas, cannot fully or properly explain it. They claim that the idea just came to them while in a meditative state, or that it came to them in a dream or vision. Some speculate about a collective universal subconscious that exists where ideas emanate from. I will discuss this theory later in the chapter.

First, we need to understand the distinction between the human brain and the human mind. "Your brain is part of the visible, tangible world of the body. Your mind is part of the invisible, transcendent world of thought, feeling, attitude, belief and imagination." The brain is the physical organ of the body that stores memories and experiences, whereas the mind, a much more complex entity, is related more to the soul of a person that controls what is done with those memories and experiences and forms an individual's personality.

Where do thoughts come from? The truth is no one knows. *I believe that thoughts come from the experiences of the body, collected by the brain, and manipulated by our minds.* I believe that thoughts emanate from, and are influenced by, the body through stimulus created while using all our senses throughout our daily lives. *Thoughts are derived from a collection of our unique experiences and associations that include use of our five senses, everything we see, hear, smell, taste, or touch.* What we associate with while using our five senses may give each one of us a different and unique thought stemming from the same sense depending on our experiences. Our brains organize the data we collect, and input, and like a computer provide a result, reaction, or output. Affect the input and you will affect the thoughts. You may smell a certain odor that transports your mind to a time in your life associated with that smell, and you will think about that time in your life. That smell triggered your brain and caused a thought. It did so because the input from your sense of smell that day was strongly associated with a high energy reaction in your body, sometimes good, sometimes bad. A built-in defense mechanism or warning from the body and mind. For me, the smell of coconut transports me back to my childhood and a very unpleasant experience on a road trip to Disney World where I indulged a little too much and became sick. To this day, I cannot eat coconut, and when I smell it, I am repulsed. Like how you influence a computer to put an idea together via inputs such as your mouse and keyboards, our brains use all five senses as inputs to create thoughts and ideas. Also, like a computer, garbage in, garbage out, if we have bad experiences and therefore bad input, we will get a bad result. A mental error akin to inputting bad data into a program. The results will not be good.

The preceding is the more traditional explanation or theory of where thoughts come from. A more controversial and unorthodox explanation or theory of where thoughts come from is that our thoughts may also be affected by primordial defense mechanisms and hereditary instincts embedded in our DNA by the evolutionary process of natural selection. Some also believe that thoughts come from outside the body and are created by external stimuli or sources, our sixth sense, an extrasensory perception, and that the brain is simply the processor of that information in the form of feelings, intuition, or hunches. There is an even a more radical and controversial theory. Have you ever heard the phrase; great minds think alike? Some believe that there is a collective and universal subconscious or information stream containing universal knowledge transmitted in waves that our brains, if trained properly, can receive, and interpret. They postulate that this is the reason how and why multiple individuals can come up with the same idea even if worlds apart or at different times. Reference *The Mind of God* by Paul Davies, chapters 6 and 9, and *Think and Grow Rich* by Napoleon Hill, chapters 6, 13, and 14. It should not be a stretch to imagine that if we can transmit information such as sounds and images wirelessly via wave packets that can then be picked up and deciphered by external receivers through electronic means, that there may not be information being transmitted into the universe by our brain waves in a similar fashion. Our brains, after all, function as a receiver of information using all of our senses that are then decoded via a series of electrical impulses that trigger synapses, which when stimulated bring about thoughts or brain waves to achieve a desired effect such as walking and talking. Think of our minds as the modems and our bodies as the electronic devices, which are powered by our brains (the computer). Some even believe that Nostradamus, Albert Einstein, and Leonardo Da Vinci, as well as other famous minds, were able to tap into this universal information stream and used information received in such a fashion to formulate their ideas and create their inventions. I have always had a fascination with universal creation and the human mind and have accumulated a substantial collection of books on the topic, ranging from the universally accepted basics of theoretical physics regarding the creation of the universe to those containing lesser accepted theories of the human mind involving the mystical realm, which science cannot explain. I leave the reader with this teaser on the subject of mysticism and recommend they do their own research on the matter and form their own conclusions. There are plenty of books available on tapping into the subconscious mind, the power of prayer and meditation, training your brain, and so on for the reader to explore. I have listed some of these books at the end of the chapter under recommend activities. However, I believe that if we come up with an original idea and do not share it or act on it, it dies with us and gets placed back into the universal knowledge stream or subconscious to await another person to draw it out. But, like with all data, when interpreted by different individuals with different experiences, it can lead to different results. Therefore, it is our duty, when we have an original thought, to act and practice on it or risk potentially losing that piece of our own individuality and legacy forever.

Next, let us discuss how to think. There are two main reasons and two main ways to think like an entrepreneur. The first reason is to *think for the purpose of coming up with ideas* and the way to do that is *by clearing your mind.* The second reason is to *think for the purpose of solving a specific problem* and the way to do that is *by focusing your mind.*

Thinking for ideas: To think properly to come up with ideas, you need to be in a relaxed state of mind far away from the distractions of life. The best way to achieve this is through meditation. It may be helpful to close your eyes and be in a dark environment. You can start by clearing your mind of all thoughts and meditating or listening to rhythmic and sooth-ing sounds. It may help to imagine and picture yourself as being caught in the jet stream or a deep ocean current. Use the image of the wind or water carrying you along to calm you and place you into the ideal state of mind for thinking. Feel the energy taking you along the path of least resis-tance. Surrender yourself to its power and let it direct your course. Focus on your breathing taking deep and long breaths as your travel along. Once you have achieved a calm state, you should then open your mind to ideas. The world has vast needs. Envision yourself on a mountain top as a wise advisor with an endless line of people bringing you their ideas to make the world a better place or in a board room as a venture capitalist listening to pitches from aspiring entrepreneurs. Focus, one by one, on those people in line and begin the dialogue with "what great idea do you have for me today?" Then, clear your mind and let your imagination or subconscious answer the question by posing that idea from each person in line and fill in the ensuing dialogue. It helps to create and generate a unique image (how they look, what they are wearing, what they sound and smell like, etc.) of each person who is posing his or her ideas for your consideration. Imagine yourself writing down all the ideas presented to you. It may take some time to get used to this, but it is a great exercise in self-control and relaxation. Only when your mind is in this relaxed state can your subconscious mind assist you in the formulation of thoughts and ideas.

Thinking to solve a problem: Once you have found your idea, the next step is to pose it in the form of questions to your subconscious mind. You need to identify a specific problem, focus your mind, and let your imagination run wild on ways to solve it. No matter how silly or absurd a solution your mind comes up with, do not shut down the process. Be prepared to jot down the ideas that come to mind by having a pen and paper ready nearby, but do not interrupt the process to do so. Let it play out. If you feel your mind wandering off, refocus it on the problem by repeating it over and over in your head. Try and focus your mind on any images that pop into your head that relate to the solution and then focus on those images.

They say you never truly forget anything you have seen or read, and it is simply safely stored away in your brain for future use. However, you must learn to tap into, and gain access to, the location where it is stored. It is like having valuable information locked away in a secure safe, if you forget the combination to the safe, you are not able to gain access to that information. The key to gaining access to that information is organization. Envision it like the filing system in your office; if you have a cluttered and messy file cabinet, it may take you some time to find what you are looking for. However, if you have a neat and organized file cabinet, you might be able to retrieve that information quite easily. Your mind works the same way, you have to organize your thoughts. The way to tap into that information and draw it out is to ask your mind for help, in the form of specific questions, and let your subconscious respond. You must be in a relaxed state to achieve the calm needed for your mind to focus on drawing out the information you have requested. Perhaps, the information you seek will be drawn from a collective subconscious that feeds us our ideas; perhaps, it is just information that we have accumulated throughout our lifetime that we have since forgotten. No one knows for sure. But, I do not doubt that ideas come to us from some sort of collective, either from our brain, the universal ether, by praying or through meditation. Call it what you will. If you learn to focus your attention and listen to your subconscious or the collective, you can solve any idea within your reach. I make it a habit, before every presentation or important meeting, to play that presentation or meeting out in my mind countless times in as many different scenarios as possible. I try to anticipate every eventuality, good or bad, and force myself to role-play how I would handle it, letting my subconscious mind fill in the dialogue. Think of it as virtual training or simulation.

Once you have learned how to think, the next step is to learn what to think about. Thinking is a key ingredient to success and how you generate ideas. *You need to understand that success begins with thoughts and thoughts turn to ideas, and if you do not stop to think or come up with ideas because you are too tired, or too busy, you cannot achieve success.*

First, and foremost, entrepreneurs think about their business. A good analogy to help you identify the most important aspects of running a business is to think of a business as a car. How do you keep your car, your ride to success, running smooth? Therefore, using that analogy, following are the top five items entrepreneurs think about, with respect to their business:

The car analogy The top five things entrepreneurs think about that affect their business		
1	The engine	The staff
2	The oil	Management
3	The spark plug	Networking
4	The fuel	Originating business
5	The wheels	Innovation

1. *How to put together a good staff.* The staff is *the engine* that runs a business. Staff includes officers, managers, professionals, and support employees. Without a good staff, the company will not produce good work. In my case, I typically assemble my staff from the top down. I look for a leader who is self-motivating and who I can trust and delegate the day-to-day operations to. I learned this lesson from reading *Rich Dad, Poor Dad*; I did not get into entrepreneurship to work harder and longer than everyone else, that, I did as an employee for many years. I got involved in entrepreneurship to work smarter and build a business with a well-trained staff that can function smoothly and let them do their job. This frees me up from the

day-to-day involvement, which in turn allows me to focus on other fruitful ventures. I train my staff leader and communicate constantly, but remotely, with them. I base my staff changes on accountability and production. I get involved mostly when I see a problem that needs correcting. A good leader who can manage their staff is essential for this type of arrangement. I am blessed to have found that combination a few times in my entrepreneurial venture. Once I find the right leader, I surround them with hard workers who are eager to learn and allow them input on staff decisions. A support staff should be versatile and work well together. I have let many staff members go due to lack of chemistry and effort. It is not easy to find the right mix, but whenever I do, and there has been much turnover, I make it a point to value them and reward them properly.

2. *How to make the company run smooth*: Management is *the oil* that keeps the engine running smooth. Company management includes managing office, cash flow, clients, projects, employees, payroll, contract workers, and profit. Without good management, the company will break down. In my case, I have a very relaxed management style that incorporates trust, but verify. I have broken down the areas of management into the preceding categories and, throughout the years, I have developed proprietary spreadsheets that allow me to analyze data regarding the company's production based on extremely specific information. I use that data to make my management decisions. Information such as: how long does it take a project to complete from the date the initial contact is made to the day the project is delivered, and every step in between? This information can help you decide which projects are more profitable. How long does it take each client to pay an invoice? This information can help you manage cash flow. Which clients ask for tasks to be performed outside of the original scope? This information can help you price a project more precisely. As an example: I analyze employee production based on billable hours versus salary to gage employee efficiency. That helps me gage the efficiency and effectiveness of each employee. I analyze project profitability by looking at fee charged versus overhead to gage the multiplier. The multiplier is "the factor by which the return deriving from an expenditure exceeds the expenditure itself."

If I charge 1,500 U.S. dollars for a service and that service costs me 500 U.S. dollars in salary to perform, not including the general overhead, that equates to a multiplier of three. That multiplier is what you will use to pay for the cost of the general overhead. This is a simple method used to understand how much to charge for your services where you can control the profit depending on market conditions, including what people are willing to pay for that service. Your overhead are the expenses incurred in performing the service, and they incorporate more than just salary expense. If your income equals your expenses, you break even, and you have a multiplier of one. Managing a business properly requires information and how you process that information, and what you derive from that information is key to how you should manage your company.

3. *How to network:* Networking is *the spark plug* that ignites the fuel to get the engine running. Without networking, the company will run out of fuel. In my case, I never really learned to network until I started my own firm. Networking is all about doing your research on a target and having a plan. It does not mean having a drink with friends at a function or conversely approaching everyone you see and blurting out what you do and asking that person if they can use your services. It requires more subtlety. It is about building a rapport, finding something in common with someone, getting to know them, and then finding a way to have a mutually beneficial working relationship. Where you network is also important. Try to target areas that will include people that you already have something in common with.

4. *How to originate business:* Originating business is *the fuel* that feeds the engine. It involves finding new clients and projects. Without originating business, the company will stall. In my case, I find that there is no substitute for face-to-face meetings. I feel that I am the best at what I do and have been doing it for some time that there is no reason that I should not be able to close the deal. Especially, since like the Godfather, I make them an offer that they cannot refuse. I guarantee to save them money without loss of quality, and in fact, with improvement of quality of service. I ask in return, that they provide me with bulk work. I can guarantee to save them money

because, I do this for only for my bread and butter work for which I can train and supervise interns to perform the work. I utilize the more experienced individuals for the more profitable projects. It is important to originate a good foundation of repeat and cookie cutter-type work to maintain a steady cash flow.

5. *How to innovate*: Innovation are *the wheels* that keep the company moving forward. Innovating means coming up with new ideas. Without innovation, the company will not move forward. In my case, I am constantly seeking to identify and implement new strategies. I am always looking to improve on existing methods or ideas. As a young engineer, I introduced computer-aided design and drafting to the firm I worked for, I updated their accounting software, streamlined their calculations and drawing templates, developed a more concise report outline, and improved communications. There is always room for improvement, you must think on it and find it.

Entrepreneurs then turn their focus to other things that affect or form part of their quest for success. An entrepreneur's way of life always seems to channel their focus back to thinking about achieving success. The top five things entrepreneurs think about to achieve success are listed as follows:

The top five things entrepreneurs think about to achieve success	
1	Their future
2	Their family and loved ones
3	How and what to invest in
4	How to build and nurture relationships
5	How to build their brand

1. *Their future*: Most entrepreneurs do not take their future for granted nor do they let outside influences dictate their future. They do not go with the flow and let life take them wherever it wants. To the contrary, they fight against external forces that lead them in a direction not conducive to success. They take control of their own future. They do this through resilience to setbacks, by understanding what is required to succeed based on examples in history, by set-

ting goals, and planning and preparing to attain them. They think about their future, lay it out in front of them, and plan it out. They ask themselves: What do I want to do with my life? How long do I want to do it for? Where do I want to be in 5, 10, or 15 years? In my case, I must break it down into before entrepreneurship and after entrepreneurship. I started my firm in 2009. Prior to that, I had not thought much about my future. Once I opened my own firm and learned what it takes to be successful, I started to take back control from the external forces that were steering my life. I created a plan, wrote it down, checked it often to gage my progress, and charged ahead. There were setbacks along the way, but I improvised, adapted, and overcame all the hurdles that threatened to derail my future goals.

2. *Their family and loved ones*: Embarking in entrepreneurship is not a one-person show. The decisions that you make will affect your family and those you love. Entrepreneurs must take that into account when making life-altering decisions and taking risks. Entrepreneurs include their families and loved ones in their decision-making process or at the very least keep them well informed and prepare them for the potential hurdles that may pop up along the way. Entrepreneurs also think of how to manage their time between work and spending quality time with their loved ones. Entrepreneurship is not a 9 to 5 job where you can clock out and forget about work, free to focus on other things. It is 24/7. Entrepreneurs think about creating a good balance between work life and family life. Part of an entrepreneur's goal with respect to their family is to ensure financial security and the time commitment involved is the price they must pay. In my case, when I became an entrepreneur, I got a lot of support from my wife. It was she who nudged me into entrepreneurship. She was by my side figuratively and financially, through the good and bad times, and there were more bad times than good at the beginning. There was financial hardship, arguments about time commitments, quarrels over consequences of my decisions that affected her, and so on. She understood that the sacrifices I was making and the decisions I was taking were taken with the best intentions regardless of the outcome. Despite the numerous quarrels, I credit her faith in me for

the success that we were able to achieve. I was even able to impart some of my entrepreneurial concepts to her, for use in her career, a successful lawyer, such as networking effectively, involvement with the community, job origination, effective communications, and so forth. She is my inspiration for success and the glue that holds my goals together.

3. *How and what to invest in*: Entrepreneurs do not like to part with their money, unless it will result in making them more money. Therefore, they are constantly thinking about money. They think about how and what to invest in to help them reach their goals and attain success. Entrepreneurs focus on opportunities and how to use other people's money to make more money for themselves. They take advantage of loans, market trends, tax deferred investments, real estate, small side business ventures, and so on. Perhaps, more importantly, entrepreneurs think about how to invest in themselves through education, their associations, their credentials, and their name. A more in-depth explanation will be provided in Chapter 6 (Focus on Investing, Not on Consuming). I keep hearing the saying that money cannot buy happiness. That is true. However, that is based on your definition of happiness. If happiness for you is living off the land, being off grid, getting by with the bare minimum, more power to you. You do not need money. Even for most of us, those who have a different definition of happiness, money still cannot buy happiness. However, our aim is not money, rather the opportunities that it can afford and the doors it can open that can lead us to our unique definition of happiness, and, most importantly, it can provide access to entrepreneurship, which can afford us the freedom to live life under our terms and not those set by other people. If you have money and are not happy, then perhaps your definition of happiness is not the right one for you. Life is full of successful yet unhappy people. In my opinion, it is not the money that made them so, it is their definition of success and their definition of happiness that has influenced their state of mind. In my case, I have invested heavily in myself by creating a name in my profession and building a brand as an expert in the hurricane mitigation field. I have done this by constantly raising awareness of my profession by

active participation in technical committees, writing articles in trade publications, presenting webinars, writing, and presenting technical papers, appearing on television news stories, podcasts, and so forth. Those efforts extend beyond my profession into the entrepreneurship realm by becoming an author on the topic who tirelessly promotes entrepreneurship and constantly is mentoring young students and professionals, presenting to student and professional organizations, judging business plan pitches, and so forth. All the aforementioned is an investment in myself and my brand. They all require time and effort. None of which, except for a few of the webinars and royalties from book sales, have I ever been compensated for. I have also invested in myself by creating credentials, based on the aforementioned efforts, that include business owner, author, expert witness, public speaker, and mentor. Aside from the self-investments aforementioned, my other investment choices have included investing in my business, my, and my wife's, 401K, and real estate. Almost all the investments involved utilizing, at least in part, other peoples' money in the forms of conventional loans, hard money loans, and credit. I always took care and analyzed to make sure the cost of the credit or loan did not outweigh the potential gains.

4. *How to build and nurture relationships*: Entrepreneurs understand that business is about building relationships and relationship are about creating bonds. Those bonds are what will develop trust between you and your clients and is what will ultimately fuel your company's growth. In most relationships, there are benefactors and beneficiaries. The benefactors provide the value and the beneficiaries derive the benefits. The best relationships, the ones that build the more solid bonds, are the mutually beneficial relationships. Ones where both sides share in the benefits. The one-sided relationships are not built on solid ground and are the ones most at risk to break down. If only one party derives benefit from their relationship with another, it will not be long until the party that does not derive the benefits seeks out a better arrangement. Entrepreneurs tend to focus on the mutually beneficial types of relationships and they make sure there is value that goes both ways. I have often heard the saying that "it's not personal, it's business." I disagree with that assertion. I think

business is personal. A client's contracts are valuable to them, they are their assets. You must build trust with your clients for them to give you their contracts. What is more personal than being entrusted with someone else's valuable assets? What I do agree with is that you must temper your emotions when doing business and never let them control your business decisions. Strong emotions, good or bad, can cloud judgment and get in the way of making smart choices. Another aspect about building relationships that entrepreneurs understand is to value all members of their client's team, not only the principals. They focus on the entire team and treat them with equal attention and respect. They understand that the associates, in time, will be the people calling the shots either at their current firm, with another firm or their own firm. Entrepreneurs understand that they will be measured by how they treat everyone, not just how they treat the principals. It is those interpersonal relationships with everyone, on the other side, that could make the difference in securing new work from individuals they dealt with in the past. Entrepreneurs also understand that building lasting relationships is heavily dependent on their level of honesty and dependability. You can be the best technical option for the job, but if you are not dependable and use whatever means is necessary to land that first job with a client and then cannot back it up, that will be the last job you get with them. Therefore, entrepreneurs think about how to best manage their relationships with their clients to develop trust and dependability, even if it means having to say no on occasion if they feel they cannot meet the clients' demands or time frames. Getting that project by whatever means necessary is good, unless you fail to deliver on your promises and then it only serves to injure your reputation. That is why, entrepreneurs think about building and nurturing their relationships with their clients. Emotional intelligence and self-awareness are extremely important in building relations and achieving success. (Read *Emotional Intelligence: Why it Could Matter More Than IQ* by Daniel Goleman.) In my case, even when I was an employee, I always made it a point to get to know everyone on a project or on a site. I did not clock out at 5 p.m., even though I could without repercussions, when I knew that a client was depending on me to meet a certain deadline. I was always honest, when asked about deadlines and most of the times I under promised and tried to over deliver. On the flip side, there have been instances where, as a consultant, I must make recommendations on which vendors to use, and even though I knew who the best vendor, technically, was, I did not recommend them because of their lack of dependability. Building and nurturing relationships is a big reason I am successful in my field today. I understood that business is personal. Two very influential books that I highly recommend you read that have inspired me in my way of thinking are: *Think and Grow Rich* by Napoleon Hill and *Rich Dad, Poor Dad* by Robert Kiyosaki. I cannot tell you how to think about all the aforementioned, that is for you to decide. I can only tell you that you must think about it and provide you with examples of how and what I thought about as an entrepreneur, in the hopes that you can derive some small measure of beneficial advice from my examples.

5. *How to build their brand*: Entrepreneurs understand that they are the brand. They think about how to promote themselves and make a name for themselves to be considered an expert in their field. Becoming known as an expert and creating credentials is key to building a good brand. One of the best ways to go about building your brand is by giving back. If you take the time to demonstrate your expertise by giving back to the community and your profession and you consider it as an investment in yourself versus seeking to be compensated for it, it will pay off in the long run. It is important to choose the right forums in which to give back. A more in-depth explanation will be provided in Chapter 12 (Create and Cultivate Your Brand) and Chapter 11 (Giving Back). In my case, I have accomplished this mostly by giving back, as mentioned in the preceding section three where I discussed self-investment.

In summary, and to answer the question: What do entrepreneurs think about? *They think about solving problems. They think about improving processes, building, and nurturing relationships, originating business, investments, building their brand, networking, innovating, and so on. They relentlessly focus their time, energy, and thoughts on any one of these problems and cling to it like a starving dog to a bone. They think about original ideas to make the world a better place, or how to improve on an already existing product or service to make it faster, better, cheaper, or more efficient. They understand the concept and the practice of thinking.*

Chapter 2: What Do Entrepreneurs Think About?

Recommended Activities

1. Learn the art of meditation.
2. Make time at least once a week to clear your mind and focus on ideas using the mountain top or venture capitalist analogies. Write those ideas down.
3. Take one of the ideas you identified from Item 2, frame it in the form of a series of specific questions and pose those questions, one by one, to your mind. Focus and meditate on how to solve them. Jot down the answers.
4. Read *The Mind of God* by Paul Davies, chapters 6 and 9.
5. Read *Emotional Intelligence: Why it Could Matter More Than IQ* by Daniel Goleman.
6. Read *Think and Grow Rich* by Napoleon Hill, chapters 6, 13, and 14.
7. Read *Rich Dad, Poor Dad* by Robert Kiyosaki.
8. Read *A Brief History of Time: From the Big Bang to Black Holes* by Stephen Hawking.
9. Study the top five items entrepreneurs think about that affect their business and start thinking about them.
10. Study the top five things entrepreneurs think about to achieve success and start thinking about them.

CHAPTER 3

What Is Entrepreneurial Mindset?

Only the limits of our mindset can determine the boundaries of our future.

This chapter will focus on the entrepreneurial way of living and answer the question of: What is entrepreneurial mindset?

Entrepreneurial mindset is composed of six main concepts and can be summarized as the art of the following:

The six main concepts of the entrepreneurial mindset	
1	Identifying and attaining goals (Chapter 4)
2	Not being afraid to take risks (Chapter 5)
3	Focusing on investing, not on consuming (Chapter 6)
4	Accumulating assets, not liabilities (Chapter 7)
5	Specializing and becoming an expert (Chapter 8)
6	Not being afraid to fail (Chapter 9)

Understanding the entrepreneurial mindset is so important that I have dedicated a complete chapter to each of the six main concepts in Part 2 of this book on *How to Act Like an Entrepreneur.*

Quite often when I speak to young aspiring entrepreneurs, I turn to my own life experiences and path to entrepreneurship as a way to bring it down to their level and motivate and inspire them to believe, that if I can do it, so can they. With that in mind, I have shared my own account of the mindset of an entrepreneur as follows:

Identifying and attaining goals: My father was a strict man, and I learned much about work ethic, responsibility, accountability, earning your way through life, paying your dues, and so on from him, more by example, than by anything else. For as long as I can remember, I had always wanted to follow his footsteps. He was my role model. He was a true entrepreneur. He had a full-time job, ran multiple businesses, was always doing things himself or would have us, his kids, do it with him, and he was not afraid to take on new challenges. All of this, after being an extraordinarily successful political figure in his home country and losing everything and being forced to start from scratch, after being exiled to the United States by a dictator. This was the foundation for what would later become my inspiration and goal in life. To become an engineer. I never had the goal of becoming an entrepreneur until later in life and, in fact, it was almost forced upon me. But, I always knew I wanted to become an engineer, and the path was not easy, but I persisted and attained my goal. It took me a little longer than most, but I did it. In fact, it almost never happened. You see, due to the strict nature of my upbringing and the tremendous responsibilities placed upon me and my older brother at such a young age, I lost accountability and lost focus on my studies. This happened shortly after my father was shot and paralyzed during a robbery attempt at one of his businesses in a dangerous part of the city in 1981 and continued through the early part of my university term. After the robbery, he was confined to the intensive care unit (ICU) and the hospital for many months, and our responsibilities, which were already great to begin with, grew even more. My father could no longer discipline us and ensure we stayed on track, and I took advantage of that fact. I did not know what to do with this new-found freedom, and it got a bit out of control. My studies suffered greatly, and my future was in jeopardy. I did not know what to do.

That is when, after finally realizing for myself that my dream of becoming an engineer was hanging by a thread (some time in 1987), I decided to meet with the associate dean of engineering at the university college of engineering. He was kind enough and understanding enough to listen to my plea, sympathize with my situation, and believe in me. He gave me a second chance, but the path he laid out for me was not easy. It was called academic bankruptcy. All my credits (I had probably accumulated enough credits to be considered a junior) were wiped out, and I would have to start all over again. Kind of what my father had to do after he was exiled, except that I was failing at the time and he had already succeeded. That individual's name is Dr. Michael

Phang, and as I wrote in the acknowledgments, I will be forever grateful for his support. The process was not easy, but I did my part and earned mostly outstanding grades going forward and obtained my degree in architectural engineering in 1996, a full 12 years after I first enrolled. I had dropped many classes during my first term, which started in 1983, taken several years off to work full time, then accepted academic bankruptcy around 1989, and went to school part time while also working part time. The reason I include this account is to show that if I can do it, if I can attain my goal, after all the mistakes, hardships, and hurdles self-afflicted or otherwise, so can anybody. Never give up on your dreams and your goals. It is never too late or too hard if you really want it and work hard to attain it.

Aside from the goal of becoming a professional, and an engineer, to be more specific, which proved to be a very challenging task due to my many setbacks and disadvantages, to say the least, I have since become much better at identifying and attaining my goals. I make it a point to write them down and date them and take actionable steps to pursue them and have had particularly good success following up and attaining many of them. Following are some of the goals that I have set out for myself, throughout my career, and life, both professional and personal, with a brief description of how I have fared to date in my pursuit of each:

Entrepreneur: President and founder of DLG Engineering, Inc. (DLGE). DLG Private Ventures, Inc. (DLGPV) and Genesis Structural Engineering, Inc. (GSE)

Real estate investor: I bought distressed properties, lived there for at least two years, and sold them for a profit: Townhouse #1 (50K plus profit), Home #1 (285K plus profit), condo hotel (46K profit), transition home (30K plus profit), townhouse #2 (90K plus profit), studio condo (10K plus profit) and one BR condo (current rental property).

Photographer: I turned a hobby in amateur photography into a philanthropic endeavor by printing my photos on aluminum and canvass and donating them to charitable organizations to be sold at silent auctions with the funds going to a worthy cause for the Cuban American Bar

Association (CABA) Art in the Tropics, Miami Bridge, Art From the Heart, and Habitat For Humanity.

Author: I took my experiences and accumulated knowledge and wrote two books on entrepreneurship: *Engineer to Entrepreneur: Success Strategies to Manage You Career and Start Your Own Firm* and this one, TAP.

Writer: I wrote magazine articles for numerous industry publications such as U.S. Glass Magazine and Architects' Guide to Glass and Metal.

World traveler: I have quite a way to go on this goal, but it is one of the more exciting ones that I have remaining, of which I am very much looking forward to. I have taken a prop plane and landed on a glacier on Mount Denali in Alaska; I have traveled to Punta Arenas (Chile) and soaked in the vistas of Torres del Paine; I have tasted the finest chocolate in Bariloche (Argentina) after river crossing the Andes mountains; I have traveled to the islands of Hawaii and seen the sunrise on Mount Haleakala; I have traveled to the Isthmus of Panama and walked on the gates of the locks of the Panama Canal; I journeyed to England and walked inside the ruins of Stonehenge; I have tasted limoncellos in Positano (Italy) and a tall glass of Guinness in Dublin (Ireland); I have stared up at the Sistine Chapel in Rome (Italy) and walked on the grounds of the Roman Colosseum; I have admired the Mona Lisa in the Louvre and gazed down on the city of lights from the Eiffel Tower in Paris (France), to name a few. This, to me, is one of the most rewarding benefits of entrepreneurship. The means and freedom to travel.

Not being afraid to take risks: Leaving my first job was difficult. I had been there for over 13 years, and it was the only discipline of engineering that I knew how to do. I was scared and did not know what to do. I set my fears aside, trusted my preparation and the knowledge I had gained, and decided to make the move. It was not easy, and I felt lost at my new job, at first. I was so afraid to fail that I offered my new boss to start me off as an entry-level engineer. I did, however, have the confidence in my work ethic that I would eventually learn another discipline of engineering and become productive. I even thought I could bring my own specialty and knowledge to the benefit of my new firm. Suffice it to say, that my fear was unfounded. Once I had established myself in that new firm, the time had come to make another move. I did not feel I was being treated fairly or properly compensated for work origination that I had brought to the firm. It was during the time of what is now referred to as the Great Recession. By this point, much of the fear and doubts of whether I can be successful had subsided, and new fears of starting my own firm and being responsible for others salary and livelihood took their place. I thought I had a good plan. I had proven that I can train a team to meet the quality of work I had been used to and that clients respected and trusted me. Suffice to say that that decision too was a good one. Another example of a huge risk, which I have recently just recovered from, involved a purchase of a high-priced condominium unit that needed a total remodel. It was to be the purchase of our dream home. This ended up being the riskiest financial decision of my career due to a series of unexpected setbacks and hurdles. The risk eventually paid off, but not after a huge financial scare, and it only paid off due to a combination of preparation and mitigation. I go into further detail about this risk in Chapter 5 on mitigating financial risk.

Focusing on investing, not on consuming: Thanks to my upbringing and my father's influence, I learned the value of money early on. I did not grow up with much money to begin with, and part of my frugality comes from having that as a foundation, but I have always looked for value in what I spent my money on. Most people are consumed with having the latest and best of everything. No pun intended. I am not built that way, and if your plan is to become an entrepreneur, and unless you come from, or have access to, wealth, you should not either. Do not even get me started on the cost of buying a nice house, new car, paying for a wedding, designer clothes, the latest electronics, and so on. I never craved the fancy car (with the exception of my very first purchase, and I still managed to keep it for 10 years), fancy house (with the exception of my last and current property, which I intend to live in for a very long time), or fancy clothes that most in society today do. I no longer accumulate material goods. I never did much, to begin with, compared to most. What I did, instead, was focus on my education, utilized my 401K, invested in a business and in real estate. I did have to furnish and decorate many rooms of all the properties that I invested in, and I must confess that I enjoyed decorating them with items I had purchased. I have owned about 12 properties in my lifetime thus far, and at one point, I owed five at one time. All of them investment properties, except for one, my homestead, which changed often. Most of the properties I invested in began as my homestead and then turned into investment properties that I rented out. I have since sold most of the investment properties and have divested most of possessions that I had accumulated, some of which remain in a storage unit. For the most part, my wife and I maintained multiple homesteads because of both coming from prior divorces with properties of our own and accounting for a blended family with rotating custody of the children. Of all the investments that I have made, starting a business has been the most rewarding. Lately, I have focused much of my spending, which I like to consider an investment in my own betterment, into travel.

Accumulating assets, not liabilities: I must credit Robert Kiyosaki, author of *Rich Dad, Poor Dad*, for this way of thinking. He made it so clear to me. Assets put money into your pocket, and liabilities take money out of your pocket. Why would you ever want to accumulate objects that take money out of your pocket? I differ a bit in his thinking of homes and cars as strictly liabilities. I believe objects can be both an asset and a liability. If you buy a car and keep it for 10 years, as I have with both of the cars that I purchased when brand new, it certainly will not appreciate, but you will save seven years of car payments, which you can use to invest and still have equity in your car when you decide to sell. If you buy the ugliest house in the nicest neighborhood, and fix it up using sweat equity over time, and make it your homestead, you will have accumulated value and appreciation with the equity in the house when you sell or if you take out an equity line. I have tried not to carry credit card debt, and if I do, it was used to invest or pay for improvements on those investments. I reduced most of my monthly liabilities to the minimum and getting by with the basics with the occasional splurge. I am content to spend my money on things that add value.

Specializing and becoming an expert: If I would have never pulled on the tiny piece of paper, in the halls of my college of engineering building, seeking clerical work for a small specialty engineering company, I may never have become an entrepreneur. After all, I was studying architectural engineering, and I wanted to design buildings. As it turned out, that clerical job exposed me to specialization. An area of engineering not even taught in school. Sure, the structural principals are the same, but the intricacies and application of them are quite different and unique. I found myself working for a small firm that I had never heard of, practicing a discipline of engineering that I never heard of. What I did come to find out was they were working on some of the most important projects in the city and for some of the biggest contractors. I stayed there for over 13 years and gained enough knowledge to become an expert in the field. That propelled me, gave me the strength and knowledge to start my own firm. That specialty also insulated me during the period starting in 2008 that has now come to be known as the Great Recession. A time when engineering firms were laying off engineers by the boat load. I was able to not only survive, but thrive by having a specialty, being the best at what I do and offering my services for cheaper while having more experience than my competitors. If it were not for that decision, to stay in that specialty, I would not be where I am today, as an expert in my field. In fact, I could very well have been one of the many highly qualified engineers that were laid off during the Great Recession, through no fault of their own.

Not being afraid to fail: Instances where I found myself close to failure include: after my father's accident when it was a difficult time in his life and mine. He was a successful business owner and entrepreneur in his own right. He was shot and paralyzed during an attempted holdup while working at one of his businesses late at night in a not-so-safe part of the city. This period tested my resolve, but I was able to overcome, and I persevered.

The time, while at the university, that I found myself at the crossroads of my life was not easy either. I had just accepted academic bankruptcy and would have to start my academic career all over again, six years after I started. I could have quit and thought about it plenty of times, but instead I persevered.

One instance that tested my perseverance and an example of how I had to improvise adapt and overcome after starting my own firm was the time, about four years in, that I lost my top three employees in the span of a few months. This occurred during what is now known as the Great Recession. The good part about the Great Recession, when it started, was the abundance of highly qualified engineers available and willing to work on a new field, to them. The bad part about the Great Recession, when it ended, was the abundance of offers those same highly qualified engineers started receiving. I had to regroup, take on huge financial losses, and rebuild my firm. But, I persevered.

Do I consider myself now to be in that latter part of that definition of an entrepreneur? Being able to do things now that most people could not by doing things earlier in life that most people would not? Yes, I believe I am. Do I consider myself successful? Yes. Have I achieved success? In the true spirit of entrepreneurship, the answer is no. No, because my definition keeps changing. There are still more mountains to climb, more problems to solve, more knowledge to be gained, more success to be had, and more goals to be attained. I would not have it any other way.

In summary, and to answer the question: What is entrepreneurial mindset? *Entrepreneurial mindset is about being resilient, chasing, and never giving up on your dreams or yourself. It is about taking risks and reaching out beyond apparent limitations. It is about investing and making sacrifices to reach your goals. It is about constantly learning and bettering oneself and becoming the best at what you do. It is about associating with like-minded individuals. It is finding ways around problems. It is about building and nurturing relationships and building and nurturing a brand. It is about not doing something just for the money and giving back to the community.*

Chapter 3: What Is Entrepreneurial Mindset?

Recommended Activities

1. Answer the following questions:
   (a) Are you ready to work hard to attain your goals?
   (b) Are you willing to act on an idea despite the risks?
   (c) Are you willing to make sacrifices now and use your money to invest instead of spending it on material goods in hope of a better future?
   (d) Are you willing to learn the difference between assets and liabilities and begin to accumulate assets?
   (e) Are you willing to study hard to become an expert?
   (f) Do you have the resilience and determination to get up after each failure and try again?
2. If the answers to the preceding questions are yes, proceed to read chapters 4 through 9 to learn how.

PART II

How to Act Like an Entrepreneur

This part of the book will focus on how to act like an entrepreneur. As detailed in Chapter 3, understanding the mindset of an entrepreneur is key to learning how to act like an entrepreneur. Entrepreneurs are not averse to making sacrifices. In fact, it might be a prerequisite. It boils down to, as I have paraphrased several times and repeat quite frequently, that an entrepreneur is someone willing to do things that most people will not for a portion of their lives in hopes of being able to do things that most people cannot for the rest of their lives.

In this part of the book, I will discuss in detail the mindset of an entrepreneur and the six main concepts that govern how he or she acts. How he or she:

1. Identifies and attains goals (Chapter 4)
2. Is not afraid to take risks (Chapter 5)
3. Focuses on investing, not on consuming (Chapter 6)
4. Accumulates assets, not liabilities (Chapter 7)
5. Becomes an expert (Chapter 8)
6. Is not afraid to fail (Chapter 9)

CHAPTER 4

Identify and Attain Your Goals

A goal identified but never attained, will
never lead to the ultimate goal, success.

This chapter will focus on exposing you to methods on how to identify your goals and then methods on how to attain your goals. It is not enough just to have goals. To be a successful entrepreneur, you not only have to identify your goals, but the next critical, and most important, step is that you need to attain your goals. A goal is defined as "the object of person's ambition or effort; an aim or desired result." Be advised, however, that goals need to be attainable, purpose-driven, lead to a specific, tangible, and meaningful end. Setting and attaining the goal of belching the alphabet, while some may consider it impressive, does not qualify as a life-altering event. Make sure that the goals you set and seek to attain, fulfill, and satisfy a deeper cause. By contrast, setting a goal of ending world hunger, while a noble cause, may not be attainable or a productive use of your time. That is not to mean that you cannot set attainable goals that follow that same path. Perhaps, identifying a goal somewhere in between setting and attaining the goal of feeding one homeless person on the one hand versus ending world hunger on the other hand. Your goals need to make sense. To identify goals that make sense, you need to identify your ultimate goal, which is success. It also makes no sense to have dreams and goals in life if you do not chase them or follow where they lead due to fear or neglect. The same philosophy applies to life goals as applies to professional goals. Goals are no different than any other living thing, in the sense that they need attention and nourishment to blossom and thrive.

Do not let your dreams and goals in life wilt and die for lack of attention. I believe it is our duty to live our lives to our fullest potential.

Goals provide you with a target, something to shoot for. They need to be specific and attainable. Goals help you narrow your focus on a specific task and obtain a specific result. There are many levels of goals in life and in your professional careers. Here, we are obviously focusing on your professional goals, with the ultimate goal being success, limited only by your imagination.

It is critical that you understand what you want out of life both personally and professionally. Your personal life will affect your professional life and vice-versa. It is hard to separate the two. For an entrepreneur, the ultimate goal is success, whatever that may be to them. The meaning of success can only be determined by yourself. It is, therefore, important to understand what your definition of success is. This will affect the quality and applicability of your goals and give them some sense. Your definition of success may be different than mine; it may even be different than your own at different points in your life. Hence, you must first define what success means for you, at this time in your life, and set your goals accordingly. Your definition of success, and therefore your goals, should form a symbiotic partnership. They should and will change together and accordingly.

There is a formula for success, but one that only you can cook up. It contains key ingredients and requires taking precise measures if you want to achieve your specific outcome. There is also a more general formula for success, which involves taking certain steps and embarking on a specific path to achieve success. It is as simple as A, B, C:

(a) Define success
(b) Identify your goals to achieve success
(c) Attain your goals and achieve success

(a) First, you must define success. Come up with your own unique definition. Find out what it means to you, currently, in your life. I cannot do this for you. No one can. But, I can help you by providing some potential ends and some potential targets. This of course will be done in the context of what this book is about, which is entrepreneurship.

You should, however, also do this for your personal life because your personal life will affect your professional life and vice-versa. Does your definition of success mean starting your own firm? Arguing in front of the Supreme Court? Finding a cure for cancer? Does it mean taking your company public? Does it mean financial independence? Does it mean obtaining the means to allow you to travel the world? Does it mean leaving behind a legacy? Does it mean being considered an expert? Does it mean obtaining the means to allow you to give back to the community in a significant way? Does it mean changing the world through your professional endeavors? Whatever it means, you must identify the appropriate definition that applies to yourself, and only then can you set and identify goals by which to achieve that version of success.

(b) Second, once you have come up with your very own definition of success, you must identify the goals that will lead you to achieve success. Goals that will facilitate a path to that end. Write them down. Identifying goals, for some people, may prove elusive. Your goals should be specific, attainable, and be set to manageable deadlines. Start by identifying your ultimate goal, based on your definition of success, and work down to smaller, attainable subgoals, with each including actionable tasks with manageable deadlines.

(c) Third, you must attain your goals and achieve success. Once you have identified your goals and ensured that they align with your specific definition of success and separated them into smaller subgoals with actionable action items associated with each, you can then set steps to attain them. Some helpful ways to assist in this is by:

1. *Writing them down and reviewing them at least once a month*: By writing your goals down on a piece of paper, you create something that you can turn to for motivation and to check your progress. At the beginning of each month, you should think about what goals you want to attain and write them down on a piece of paper and date it. At the end of the month, you can then pull it out and review your progress and either check off or modify your goals.

2. *Building a success box to store your goals*: By creating and labeling a box in which to place your goals in it gives you something to draw

attention to that cannot be lost or misplaced. Unlike with a piece of paper stuck inside a notebook, every time you see the box, it will remind you of your goals.

3. *Rewarding yourself when you achieve a goal*: By rewarding yourself when you achieve a goal, it creates a positive reinforcement. Rewarding yourself can create motivation and incentive to work harder to attain your goals.

4. *Being ready to act when opportunities become available*: By having identified your goals in advance, you should be well prepared to take advantage of any opportunities that may present themselves so that you can act quickly and decisively. Advanced preparation will mitigate the potential to miss out on such opportunities.

5. *Being open minded to course corrections*: By keeping an open mind, you put yourself in a position to best determine if the goals you have set for yourself are the most appropriate. You should always review your goals to make sure they make sense as you mature and grow. It makes no sense to strive for a goal that is no longer relevant. Your goals should change as your definition of success changes.

Planning for, and achieving, success is not that much different than writing a book. For those of you who have not written a book, the process can be summarized in five steps, as follows:

The book biography analogy The five steps to achieve success		
1	Identify your topic:	Define success.
2	Title it appropriately:	Identify your ultimate goal.
3	Develop an outline of chapters:	Break it down into smaller goals.
4	Fill in the substance of chapters:	Accumulate knowledge.
5	Publish your work:	Put that knowledge to practice.

Using the analogy of writing a book and following the outline of that book on how to achieve success, as an actual means to achieve success, is the best way I know of to teach you how to attain your goals. Consider it foreshadowing your future. As the author of your own life, you will have a lot of control, but you will be dependent on the editors (teachers) and publishers (partners) and contributors (friends and family) to achieve success and make it a bestseller. For this example, I have used the definition of success of becoming an entrepreneur, which after all, is the main premise of this book. However, feel free to substitute in your own definition of success and adjust accordingly. Start by:

1. *Identifying your topic*: Come up with your unique definition of success, what success means to you.
   (a) Becoming an entrepreneur
2. *Titling it appropriately*: Identify your ultimate goal; the one that will get you to that end.
   (a) Owning my own business
3. *Developing an outline of chapters*: Identify smaller attainable goals that will eventually lead to your ultimate goal, based on your unique definition of success.
   (a) Chapter 1: Read a good book on entrepreneurship (hint, hint!).
   (b) Chapter 2: Identify your specialty or niche and become an expert.
   (c) Chapter 3: Find ways to fund your start-up costs.
   (d) Chapter 4: Learn about company start-up logistics.
   (e) Chapter 5: Incorporate your business.
   (f) Chapter 6: Learn about office logistics.
   (g) Chapter 7: Learn about marketing, communications, and networking.
   (h) Chapter 8: Learn about business management.
   (i) Chapter 9: Learn to grow your company.
   (j) Chapter 10: Learn to give back.

Not coincidentally, I have taken much of the preceding outline straight out of my first book on entrepreneurship titled *Engineer to Entrepreneur: Success Strategies to Manage You Your Career and Start Your Own Firm* (e2E). I highly recommend you read it because it contains many of the actual chapters previously cited, with many of the concepts of how to prepare for, start, and manage your own firm, down to the details of tax implications, funding sources, incorporation, and so on. It is an excellent companion reference book to this one.

4. *Filling in the substance of the chapters*: Accumulate the necessary knowledge. Set the foundation for and path to attaining your goals and fulfilling your dreams. Follow the outline you set out for yourself. Begin accumulating all the knowledge and experience required. Draw on the information gathered based on life experiences and knowledge gained from research or available resources. Learn to tap into the collective subconscious. Find inspiration and utilize meditation techniques.

5. *Publishing your work*: Open your own business. This is where you put all your ideas to practice. At this point, you will have persevered, paid your dues, become an expert, and embarked on the voyage that is entrepreneurship. It makes no sense to have a great idea and not following up on it, for whatever reason, acting on it and putting it to practice. It would be considered a waste.

You can utilize this same method to identify your version of what success is in all aspects of your business or venture. Such as finding a specialty, improving a product or service, identifying needs, developing a new product, taking your company public, and an endless number of other goals. Coming up with unique ideas and goals requires foresight, creativity, and a knack for innovation. You should practice thinking and mediating on coming up with ideas and learning to tap into the collective subconscious, as explained in Chapter 2.

Do not be afraid to open your mind to the possibility of *divine intervention* in your life. This divine intervention may be able to steer you in a new direction or inspire a change in you. It might affect how, when, and what ideas come to you if you learn how to listen for, and to, them. I often think of my father's influence after a particularly good result in a business venture or investment that I had no idea how I came to attain. Of course, it occurred based on research, hard work, and determination, nonetheless, I do believe his spirit is guiding and looking out or me. Perhaps, still influencing and inspiring me.

Some of the more specific goals that I have identified for myself and attained are listed next as are some that are still a work in progress:

1. Buying my first house…check

2. Starting my own firm...check

3. Investing in real estate...check

4. Selling my first photo art piece...check

5. Writing and getting my first article published...check

6. Writing a book...check

7. Becoming a public speaker...check

8. Becoming a mentor...check

9. Becoming an expert witness...check

10. Traveling to all 50 states...work in progress

11. Writing my second book...work in progress

12. Obtaining my Professional Engineer (P.E.) certification.... work in progress

Chapter 4: Identify and Attain Your Goals

Recommended Activities

1. Identify what makes you happy. See Chapter 14, section on self-awareness.
2. Define what success means to you based on your unique definition of happiness.
3. Identify your ultimate goal based on your definition of success.
4. Identify the subgoals that will lead you to attain your ultimate goal.
5. Develop a specific timeline with action items for each subgoal.
6. Write down your ultimate goal, along with your itemized subgoals, date them, and place them in a box.
7. Return to review and modify your timelines and/or goals every month or as often as needed.

CHAPTER 5

Do Not Be Afraid to Take Risks

Exposing yourself to the chance of injury or loss in the pursuit of betterment is a key entrepreneurial trait.

This chapter will focus on the concept of risk and how to mitigate it. Risk is defined as: "exposure to the chance of injury or loss." The biggest deterrent to entrepreneurship, aside from the start-up funding aspect, is fear, and avoidance, of risk. The first part of that combination, fear, is natural, and you can learn to channel it. Fear is a great motivator. Use its energy to fuel you to prepare better, practice harder, study more, and think longer. The second part, avoidance, is counterproductive. It means you are not confronting or dealing with an issue. You are foregoing a potential means of growth and experience. Do not avoid risk, learn to mitigate it. Learning to mitigate risk can make you a better person. It can teach you valuable lessons about yourself and expose areas that need improvement.

Exposing yourself to the chance of injury or loss is to make yourself vulnerable. But, like with any other practice, the more you expose yourself to an action, or the more your practice to prevent injury or loss, the more you get used to it and the better you learn to deal with it. Like the basketball player who takes 1,000 shots from the same spot to prepare himself or herself for the pressure of the potential moment and increase his or her chances of success. He or she never would have experienced that euphoric moment, of taking the winning shot, if he or she had avoided the situation and passed the ball at that critical time for fear of loss. Most of us are taught by society and our family to fear or avoid risk. Risk is not a bad thing, and it is not your enemy. Consider risk as a challenge waiting to be conquered. Without risk, many of our greatest ideas would never have been put to practice, and we would have been deprived of some of our biggest successes and accomplishments. Like with our country's space program, where they faced many risks involved in reaching for and attaining the goal of landing on the moon, where lives were at stake. The risks of harm or loss were present to all involved, but that did not stop them. They prepared, planned, tested, researched, and pushed forward, despite the risks. If our scientists would have avoided those risks, there would never have been that iconic moment our country is so proud of.

It is also not a wise idea to take unnecessary risk or risk without preparation or potential reward. Treat risk as an investment in yourself. Think of risk as a journey to self-improvement. There must be a thoughtful meaning and reason to expose yourself to harm or loss. Thoughts and actions should be forever linked. You should not do one without the other. Do not let risk become an obstacle to success. If you do not act on your ideas and take advantage of opportunities that present themselves for fear and avoidance of risk, you will never reach your true potential. It also does not mean to act on just any idea or jump at any chance you get. All opportunities need to be carefully thought out, planned, and then acted upon. There is a saying that I use often, *do not act without thinking and do not think without acting.*

There are two main types of risk for entrepreneurs, and three main ways mitigate each. The two main types of risks are financial and emotional. Next, I will show you the three ways to mitigate each:

Financial risk: Exposure to financial losses:

1. *Prepare*: The best way to mitigate risk is to be prepared. Understand the difference between good and bad risks. Do not take unnecessary or undue risk. A good risk is one that falls in your area of expertise and offers a significant reward at the end that greatly outweighs the consequences of failure. A bad risk is one that falls outside your area of expertise and offers a minimal reward at the end that does not measure up to the consequences of failure. To be prepared to take risks, good ones, you must thoroughly understand the subject matter. It is like preparing for a test. If you listen in class, do the homework assignments, and read the assigned books, the odds are in your favor that you will pass. The same is true of preparing for

risks. Perform a risk assessment. Do your research and homework and understand what you are getting yourself into. Make a list of the consequences and potential losses involved of taking the risk. On the one hand, list all the potential consequences associated with failure, on the other hand list all the potential consequences associated with success. Take an accounting and judge if the risk is worth the reward. However, be advised that by the very nature of risk, no amount of preparation can ensure success, you can only hope to maximize the gain or minimize the loss. You can also turn a bad risk into a good one through preparation. In my case, I have experienced both sides of the preparation equation. I have recollections of where I too often entered a classroom unprepared for a test and suffered the consequences early in my academic career. I also have memories of entering a client meeting well prepared with confidence, fully expecting to get the project or contract. Preparation truly is the best way to mitigate risk.

2. *Accumulate assets*: The second-best way to mitigate risk is to limit your exposure to risk. As most of the risks associated with entrepreneurship involve exposure to financial losses, you should prepare yourself by fortifying your tolerance to loss. You can do this by accumulating assets and distributing them accordingly based on your risk assessment. There are two types of assets, liquid and fixed. Liquid assets are cash or those assets that are easily and readily converted into cash. Fixed assets are long-term investments that are not readily converted into cash. You will want to assess your liquid assets and possibly liquidate some of your fixed assets in preparation for your upcoming exposure. In my case, an accumulation of assets became a lifeline for me in one of the toughest financial stretches of my career. I was burdened with a series of unfortunate events that made meeting my financial obligations nearly impossible. If it were not for that accumulation of assets, which I was able to liquidate and use as a lifeline, I fear bankruptcy and foreclosure may have been inevitable. I started this story back in Chapter 3 regarding the riskiest financial decision of my career. I had taken a huge risk, planned well, but was struck by unexpected hurdles and setbacks. It involved a risky purchase of a high-priced condominium unit that needed a total

remodel. It was to be the purchase of our dream home. The problem was that it was being sold at auction, and only cash buyers could bid. We did not have that kind of cash, so I sought out a short-term hard money lender to provide the cash and remodel funds. The purchase would have to be done through a limited liability company that I owned so that the hard money lender could foreclose and take title of the property if I could not repay the short-term loan. That is the only way they would lend me the money. My plan was to purchase the property using the cash from the hard money loan and remodel it, then transfer title via a quit claim deed from my limited liability company to my name to then be able to secure a conventional mortgage and repay the hard money lender after the remodel was complete. It was a good plan, but the process quickly veered away from the plan. I secured the hard money loan, won the bid, but not after a competing bidder drove the price of the property higher than I had planned to pay. That was the *first hurdle*. The *second and third hurdles* occurred upon appraisal, when the property, in its existing condition, did not appraise to the satisfaction of the hard money lender, which then subsequently reduced the amount of remodel funding that I had originally requested and been approved for, contingent on appraisal, of course. Therefore, I had to find another source of funding to complete the remodel. Due to the low appraisal and reduced remodel funds made available to me, I ended up maxing out our credit cards to complete the remodel. A series of construction cost overruns and permit delays became the *fourth and fifth hurdles*, which stretched the hard money loan terms to its limit and further strained our credit limits and cash flow. This was the *sixth hurdle* I had not counted on. If we could not finish the remodel and close out the permit, the bank would not lend us the money to repay the hard money loan, and we would default and risk losing the property. Having strained every inch of available credit and using up all of our available cash, we managed to complete the remodel, quit claim deed the property to our names, secure a conventional loan, and repay the hard money lender. However, not without encountering further problems and hurdles. Once again, the completed property did not appraise as expected, and the bank refused our request for an equity line of credit that would have allowed us to pay off our credit card debt, which we had incurred to complete the remodel. That became the *seventh hurdle.* We were now saddled with maxed-out credits cards at extremely high interest rates, but we were still within our means to repay. That is when the *eighth and costliest hurdle* reared its ugly head. Our taxes, due to the major upgrade in the condition and value of the property, tripled, but the bank did not account for that increase and grossly underestimated our escrow payments, and we now had a significant shortage in our escrow reserve, which immediately caused our mortgage payments to double to make up for the escrow shortage. We now found ourselves unable to meet all our financial obligations, and we let our credit card payments slip so that we could meet our mortgage obligation. To add insult to injury, three months after we closed on our newly remodeled unit, we encountered our *ninth and tenth hurdles* when we were struck hard by hurricane IRMA, which caused significant water damage to our newly remodeled unit. The insurance company initially offered us a total of approximately 900 U.S. dollars to repair the damage. We had to sue the insurance company and had to litigate it for over one year, to get a fair settlement. As it turned out, we had accumulated assets for such an eventuality. We had numerous investment properties that we owned, and it was not my plan to do so, but we managed to liquidated three of them and used the cash to pay off most of our debt to relieve ourselves from the financial hardship we were facing. My original plan was to secure a hard money loan, including funds to complete a total remodel, purchase the property with cash at auction, remodel the unit, quit claim the unit to our names, and secure a conventional loan with an additional equity line of credit, which we would use to pay off the remodel costs. I had done my homework. I had a planned it out. I understood the risks involved. I had accounted for them, or so I thought. I was accustomed to the sacrifices involved once the plan went south, my wife, not so much. However, because I had accumulated those assets, lowered our liabilities, and planned for the risks, we were able to overcome. We persevered. We now live in that beautiful unit, to this day, and cherish every minute of our time in it for its exquisite views and the peace that it brings us. The moral of this story is that if I had not had an accumulation of assets as mitigation for this very situation, I may not have been writing this book from my new condo unit with a great view. Because of that mitigation strategy, we now we find ourselves in a good financial situation once again.

3. *Reduce liabilities*: Another way to limit your exposure to losses is to reduce your liabilities and expenses. Review your budget. Cut down on all unnecessary expenses while you undertake the risk. Build yourself a financial cushion or safety net. In my case, prior to any potentially life-altering event (purchase of a home, change in jobs, launching my company), I always made sure to review our expenses and reduce them to the bare essentials to help mitigate any unforeseen financial situations. This was especially true in the prior example, and most recently, during the global pandemic COVID-19 that affected the entire world. I was able to understand and anticipate the need for us to tighten belts and reduce expenses and prepare for most eventualities to give ourselves the best chance to succeed and survive. I go into more detail on how preparation, accumulation of assets, and reducing liabilities helped us through the global pandemic COVID-19 in Chapter 11.

Emotional risk: Exposure to mental or reputational injury:

1. *Be open with your family and loved ones*: Taking a risk does not only involve exposure to financial loss; it also could involve exposure to mental or reputational injury. The risks involved with entrepreneurship, whether they be exposure to financial loss or exposure to mental or reputational injury, are not borne by you alone. They are carried by your family and loved ones as well. Talk openly about the upcoming risks and how you have planned for them. Discuss the sacrifices you will be expected to make. Being open about the hardships and struggles you can face, or are facing, is one way to lessen the emotional burden. Do not hide those feelings from your family or loved ones. In my case, I learned this lesson a bit later in the game, and my hope is that an aspiring entrepreneur will take heed of this

advice. Refer to Chapter 8, the piece on the perspective of the significant other of an entrepreneur for more helpful advice on the topic.

2. *Create an advisory group*: Entrepreneurs understand that they do not know everything, so they surround themselves with advisors in all fields of practice to consult and seek advice from. This will help mitigate potential risk by filling in the knowledge gaps that could lead to mistakes. Entrepreneurs know that they cannot go at it alone, and that they need help from professionals, who are well versed in the areas they lack knowledge in, to keep them out of trouble, especially in the fields of law and accounting and taxation. Risk does not just include exposure to financial losses or mental injury or stress, but it also could include injury to your reputation. Having a group of knowledgeable advisors can help mitigate potential injury to mental health and reputation. In my case, I always made it a point to pick the brains of all my professional advisors and not just take their advice without first knowing why. I would then practice due diligence and read up on the topics to gain a better understanding.

3. *Create a support group*: Risks cause stress, and stress causes anxiety, and that can lead to mental injury. You should not underestimate the power of stress and the effects it can have on your well-being. Like with any other potentiality, you need to be prepared to handle the stress associated with being a business owner and responsible for the financial well-being not only of yourself but of your employees and staff. Do not be afraid to ask for help. You should identify people who you can talk to, preferably someone who has faced what you are facing. In my case, part of the reason I wrote this book is that I found few available resources regarding the struggles of entrepreneurship, what that entailed, and how to overcome them, so my hope is to mitigate that for the reader by providing this book as a reference and resource.

Chapter 5: Do Not Be Afraid to Take Risks

Recommended Activities

1. List all the fears you have and your reasons for avoiding them.
2. Write down the potential injury or loss.
3. Write down the potential benefits.
4. Make a risk assessment by comparing the potential injury or loss versus the potential benefit and decide if it is a good risk to take.
5. Make a list of ways to mitigate each of the risks and potential injuries and form a mitigation strategy for the future for each.

CHAPTER 6

Focus on Investing, Not on Consuming

To focus on investing is to contribute to your future, to focus on consuming is to contribute to others' futures.

This chapter will focus on the art of investing and the limiting of consumption. It will go hand in hand with Chapter 7 on accumulating assets, and not liabilities. To invest is defined as: "to expend money" (I would add effort) "with the expectation of achieving a profit or material result." To consume is defined as: "to use up" or "to buy." We will not, however, be discussing the stock market or the benefits of bonds versus stocks in this chapter or in the book in general. What we will focus on is how to invest and what to invest in if entrepreneurship is your goal. We will be discussing investing in things that add value to your life. Investing in things that increase your net worth. Investing in things that put you in a better position to achieve success. Investing should not be limited to material things only; it should include learning to invest in yourself.

This chapter will also caution you to avoid overconsumption. The art of consumption, or better said, overconsumption, adds value to others net worth and others' lives, not yours. Of course, we need to consume goods and services to live, but entrepreneurs learn to limit the amount and type of consumption they participate in.

To become an entrepreneur, it is not necessary to make a lot of money. What is necessary and critical is your investment philosophy and what you do with the money you make. Consider the example of a high-wage earner who focuses on consumption versus an average-wage earner who focuses on investing and limiting consumption. You can be an extremely high-wage earner and your net worth, over time, could be less than an average-wage earner, over the same time span, simply due to your investment philosophy. Take the example of two recent graduates straight out of college, a high-wage earner that makes 100,000 U.S. dollars per year in income, call them earner A, versus and average wage earner that makes 50,000 U.S. dollars per year in income, call them earner B.

Earner A: Earner A has the mindset of a consumer. Earner A decides to rent a nice condo in a nice neighborhood right after graduation. They decide to forego contributing to their 401K. They lease a nice car every three years, party every weekend, buy designer clothes and the latest gadgets. They rely heavily on their credit cards whenever they run short of cash at the end of the month and accumulate liabilities. *Earner A, due to their life-style choice with a focus on consuming, lives paycheck to paycheck where their monthly expenses equal or exceed their monthly income and have accumu-lated liability in the form of credit card debt used on their consumables. After six years, they decide to look at their net worth.* They have no liquid assets because they have lived paycheck to paycheck since they graduated, and they have no money put away in their 401K. They have no fixed assets because they decided to rent their apartment. They have accumulated liability in the form of credit card debt and car lease payments. They have no investments, including not investing in themselves, because they spent all their weekends and spare time having fun. *Earner A realizes that they have a negative net worth (their liabilities are greater than their assets).* They have no assets and instead have accumulated liabilities for the six years since they graduated college. If they were to lose their job, they would have no assets (liquid or fixed) to fall back on, and instead they have bills to pay on their liabilities, including their condo rent payments, that they can no longer afford.

Earner B: Earner B has the mindset of an investor. Earner B decides to live at home with their parents for three years while they set money aside for a down payment on fixer upper condo in a nice neighborhood. They decide to max out their 401K contributions each year, which their employer matches. They buy a modest car that they have kept for the last six years, which they paid off in three years, leaving them with no car payments for the last three years. Those savings allow them to put that money aside to invest. They use their weekends to make extra money on a side business, do not focus on consuming expensive clothes or gadgets, and use their credit and loans to accumulate assets. *Earner B, due to their lifestyle choice with a focus on investing, sets aside money each month after budgeting their expenses and has utilized their credit to use on investment ventures. After six years, they decide to look at their net worth.* Their liquid assets include plenty of cash in their bank account from their side job, as well as setting money aside each month since they graduated, and their 401K balance has grown significantly because of tax deferred investments and matching contributions from their employer. Their fixed assets include their new condo, which they purchased three years after graduation with the savings they made by living with their parents for three years and a loan from their 401K. Their condo has increased in value after three years of making steady improvements using sweat equity, giving them positive equity in their property. The cost of their mortgage is less than the average cost of renting a unit in their neighborhood since they bought a fixer upper at a greatly reduced price. They have a small liability in the form of credit card debt, which they used to fix up their condo. They have no car payments. Their side business has grown, and they have improved themselves by taking classes on the weekends and investing in themselves. They do a tally of their assets (cash in the bank, cash in his 401K, earnings from their side business, equity in their condo), and they far outweigh their liabilities. *Earner B realizes they have a positive net worth.* If they were to lose their job, they would be well positioned to weather the storm, and in fact, they have plans to start their own firm. Now, imagine if both made the same money out of college. The example of Earner A is not uncommon nor is it a stretch. Unfortunately, it is more of the norm than the exception. The example of Earner B, embodies, mostly, the philosophy that I have employed in my career and is what I consider to be the entrepreneurial mindset put to practice. Living the entrepreneurial lifestyle and adopting that mindset takes sacrifice and discipline, but if done faithfully and correctly, it will pay off greatly in the long run.

To attain your goal of becoming an entrepreneur, you need to invest the money you earn, regardless of the amount, wisely. As previous stated, you do not need to make a lot of money to become an investor. The seven best investment vehicles for entrepreneurs are as follows:

The seven best investment vehicles for entrepreneurs	
1	Invest in yourself
2	Invest in assets
3	Invest in real estate
4	Invest in and max out your 401K
5	Invest with other people's money
6	Invest in collectibles
7	Invest in your employees

1. *Invest in yourself*: The best investment vehicle to focus on is to invest in yourself and in your own future. Make it a point to invest in your education and continually learn and improve yourself. Make decisions and set goals to increase your self-worth. Invest in people who will help make you a better person. Read up on people from your contemporary life and from history and study how they acted. Surround yourself with people who are smarter than you and soak it all up.

2. *Invest in assets*: The second-best investment vehicle is to focus on compound investing. Investments that lead to investments. One such investment vehicle is investing in a business venture. It does not have to be a business that encompasses or leads you to your ultimate goal, depending at what stage in life you are. It can be a business that puts money into your pocket. Money that you can then use to invest in other things, that put more money into your pocket, to then invest on other things, and so on. After all, it is never too early to prepare for and plan to be an entrepreneur. You can start as early as high school or college. Ventures such as a tutoring business, a lawn care business, a lemonade stand. Anything that puts a skill you possess into practice. Something that will provide you with extra income to further invest with and afford you experience in running a business. A dry run at entrepreneurship.

3. *Invest in real estate*: The third-best investment vehicle is to invest in real estate. Learn how to buy your homes wisely. Focus on buying the ugliest house in the nicest neighborhood. By doing so, buying a fixer upper, you are investing in a good neighborhood, ensuring demand, but you are buying in at a cheaper price than your neighbors due

to the condition of the house. Therefore, your liability (mortgage, interest expense, and taxes) will be much lower than your neighbors. Also, by being in a nice neighborhood, you guarantee an increase in equity over time if you make improvements to your house little by little through sweat equity focusing on the kitchens, bathrooms, and curb appeal (fresh paint and new landscaping). After a minimum of two years (the time threshold to be exempt from being taxed on the profit or capital gains on the sale of a homestead property or primary residence) of making small improvements to bring your house up to par with the rest of the neighborhood, your house will be more valuable, and if you look at the comparable sales in your neighborhood, your house would have also increased in value by association as well. Now, when you sell your home, you can realize that gain in the form of tax-free profit and utilize that to do the same thing over and over every two years, buying a bigger and bigger house, all fixer uppers, of course. As an example, let us say you buy an ugly fixer upper house for 300,000 U.S. dollars in a nice neighborhood where the comparable sales are between 350,000 and 400,000 U.S. dollars. During the two years that you live there, you invest 15,000 U.S. dollars to update the kitchen and bathrooms and another 5,000 U.S. dollars to paint the house inside and out plus redo the landscape. You now have a total investment in the property of 320,000 U.S. dollars. After two years, all the houses have appreciated in value about 5 percent each year (in a good market). So, now the homes are worth between 385,500 and 440,000 U.S. dollars. If you sell your house at the average comparable sale of 412,500 U.S. dollars, you potentially stand to make 92,500 U.S. dollars in gross profit that after closing cost (5,000 U.S. dollars) and sales commission (6 percent, 24,750 U.S. dollars) can net you 62,750 U.S. dollars total profit or about 31,000 U.S. dollars per year profit. Again, it is not easy to buy an ugly house and live in it while making the improvements, but it is a proven way to make a lot of money in real estate if you can handle the sacrifice involved. Whereas this example is a hypothetical, the strategy is not. I have personally utilized this strategy to my advantage many times.

4. *Invest in and max out your 401K:* The fourth-best investment vehicle and the best, absent all the aforementioned, is to invest in and max

out your 401K. By investing in your 401K, you are taking advantage of a tax-deferred investment vehicle that can increase in value over time if you learn how to manage it properly. Even more so if your company matches your contributions. The way to manage it properly is to follow the simple adage of buy low, sell high. The stock market is cyclical, and it will always fluctuate between high and low in the long term. It will also undertake large short-term fluctuations influenced and caused by current events. It amazes me how such a simple, tried and true principle is so misunderstood or disregarded by so many. Most people are triggered by euphoria and panic. During the long-term fluctuations, when the market is high and doing good, euphoria sets in and everyone jumps on the bandwagon, and they buy. When the market is low and not doing well, panic sets in and everyone jumps off the bandwagon, and they sell. The smart thing to do, during long-term fluctuations, which requires very little knowledge of the stock market (most 401K's offer mostly mutual funds) and if you have many years of employment left, is to buy when the market is low and sell when the market is high. You should always have a balance in your 401K account of high and low-risk investments. During large short-term fluctuations that are influenced by current events, there is an opportunity to take advantage of the panic and make a lot of money in a short period of time you if know what to look for. Most 401K plans offer all the information that you need to make an informed decision on the mutual funds you want to invest in, including price per share and historical performance over time. The key is to select a few mutual funds and become intimately familiar with what they invest in and track their performance over time. This can be easily done using free online services that track mutual fund performance. When the stock market takes a big tumble, after an unusual current event occurrence, you need to quickly see how the mutual funds you invest in have been affected. If a particularly well-performing mutual fund suddenly drops five U.S. dollars per share overnight, you have a tremendous opportunity to buy low and wait for it to recover and realize a large gain. You simply take some of the money you have in your low-risk investments and transfer them into that mutual fund that just dropped five U.S. dollars per share. It is particularly important for you to know what the mutual fund invests in to make sure it is just a panic selloff and not a major problem with the investments that make up most of the mutual fund investments. As an example, let us say that there is a highly rated and particularly good-producing mutual fund that has steadily been increasing in value for a few years and stands currently at 15 U.S. dollars per share. News comes out of a terrorist attack on an oil installation in a foreign country and the stock market drop 500 points overnight and set off a panic selloff. You look at the mutual fund and it has dropped five U.S. dollars per share overnight and it now stands at 10 U.S. dollars per share. If you move money from your low-risk mutual funds or even a safer money market fund, which, by definition, would not have dropped as much or been affected by the selloff, and you buy 500 shares of that mutual fund at 10 U.S. dollars per share (5,000 U.S. dollars), the odds are in your favor that is less than one week, when the panic subsides, that same mutual fund will recover all its losses and continue on its upward trend. If it recovers fully back to the postpanic price of 15 U.S. dollars per share, you would have realized a 2,500 U.S. dollars gain in less than one week. Whereas this example is a hypothetical, the strategy is not. I have personally utilized this strategy to my advantage many times, including during the stock market crash of 2020 as a result of the global COVID-19 pandemic. When the market crashed and most people were selling their stocks at rock-bottom prices, I was doing my research and I started buying mutual funds, using money set aside in safer investments, that invested in the hard-hit cruise line industry. Their stocks had suffered catastrophic losses, and I saw the potential for a relatively quick rebound when the panic subsided. As of the time of the writing of this section, I had managed to realize a 55,000 U.S. dollars gain on our mutual fund portfolio from where it stood prior to the pandemic. Most 401K portfolios were either recovering their losses, for those who stayed in, or had cemented their losses, for those how sold out. I managed to do this without extensive knowledge of the stock market, simply by following the adage of buy low, sell high, and understanding the emotional components of euphoria and panic involved in buying and selling stocks after a traumatic event, not associated with a regular stock market inflection point. Another way to utilize your 401K is to, when you start your own firm and become the administrator of your own 401K, set up the option of taking out loans for whatever reasons without restrictions. You will have to offer that option to your employees as well. Once you have done that, you can then roll over your entire balance from your former employers account, without incurring any tax consequences, into you own plan. You now have access to a maximum of 50,000 U.S. dollars *interest-free* loan. You will have to set up a repayment plan, but the interest gets put back into your own account, and you are free to set up your own terms, as the administrator. This is not a hypothetical example; I have personally utilized this strategy to my advantage.

5. *Invest with other people's money*: The fifth-best investment vehicle involves using other people's money to make money for you. Such as learning to properly utilize loans, credit, and investors. When utilizing loans or credit and seeking out investors, you need to understand what the cost of the loan or credit will be, such as the terms and interest rates, and gage whether the investment will not only cover the costs, but put you in a better capital or equity position afterward. Using loans and credit is a good way to invest in things when you do not have the liquid assets or capital on hand or when your available capital or assets are being effectively utilized in other areas to increase your net worth. You should never limit your potential gains by your available liquid assets. Seek out more means of borrowed capital to invest wisely.

6. *Invest in collectibles*: The sixth-best investment vehicle for entrepreneurs is to invest in collectibles that appreciate over time. This is a good way to build and increase your net worth, which in turn provides you with more money to invest. Examples of collectibles include precious metals, art, antiques, and precious stones.

7. *Invest in your employees*: The seventh-best investment vehicles to invest in, and perhaps the most important one for your business, is to invest in your employees. When you become an entrepreneur, you must remember to invest in your employees, your company, and your brand. Train, delegate, and allow other people to work for you

and make money for you. Surround yourself with trustworthy people and allow them to do their job. Make sure your staff is constantly growing and expand their marketable skills. Make them feel vested in your company and your brand. Nothing enhances a brand more than pride emanating from your staff, which is reflected onto your clients.

Chapter 6: Focus on Investing, Not on Consuming

Recommended Activities

1. Review your spending and identify how much money you are spending monthly and yearly on luxury items or services that are non-essential.

2. Add up that money and investigate how alternatively you might be able to invest that amount of money.

3. Identify investment targets and how much capital, time, and energy it would take to realize a positive return on investment.

4. Identify all possible forms of loans, credit, or investors for each potential investment target.

5. Find ways that you can improve yourself (classes, certifications, experiences, books to read, and so on) that would be helpful to your career and actively pursue them.

6. Find a way to improve your employees' worth to themselves (training, certification, experience, and so on) that will also benefit your company.

CHAPTER 7

Accumulate Assets, Not Liabilities

Having nice things in life is a reality one should strive for, it should not be an illusion created for self-gratification.

This chapter will focus on the differences between assets and liabilities and show you how, by accumulating assets and reducing liabilities, you can increase your net worth. This scenario was demonstrated by the example in Chapter 6 (Focus on Investing, Not on Consuming) between Earner A and Earner B. The same item, acquired differently or under different circumstances, can be considered either an asset or a liability. Learn to tell the difference. Accumulating assets and reducing liabilities can also serve as a backup plan or safety net for potential financial hardships. Assets come in two main types: liquid and fixed. Liabilities also come in two main types: loans and expenses. An asset is defined as: "a useful or valuable thing person or quality." A liability is defined as: "the state of being responsible for something or a person or thing whose presence or behavior is likely to put one at a disadvantage." For the purpose of this chapter, we will define an asset as anything that increases in value over time or puts money in your pocket and anything that decreases in value over time or takes money out of your pocket as a liability. Assets and liabilities can be tangible or intangible, objects or people, even behaviors or qualities. An accumulation of assets provides you with more weapons for your battle against the obstacles of entrepreneurship and potential hardships, whereas an accumulation of liabilities just adds more obstacles and can exacerbate the hardships. Assets and liabilities consist of:

1. *Liquid assets: Cash or cash equivalent:* Cash on hand, cash in checking or saving account, money market account, certificates of deposit,

trust fund, cash surrender value on insurance policy, inheritance, 401K loan potential. All of these items are, or can be, readily converted to cash.

2. *Fixed assets*: Items that have monetary value that cannot be readily converted to cash. Items such as real estate, vehicles, loans made to others, personal property, long-term investments, and so on.

3. *Loans or debts*: These are your main forms of liabilities. Car loan or lease, house mortgage or rent, credit card debt, student loans, monthly living expenses (utilities, phone, water, cable)

4. *General investments:* Investments, either tangible or intangible, should be chosen with the specific goal in mind of accumulation of worth. Does your investment in that product, service, or relationship lead to increased worth? If it does, it is an asset; if it does not, it is considered a liability.

5. *Consumables or personal possessions*: Items that you buy or use up. They can be considered either assets or liabilities, but are mostly liabilities. We, of course, must consume goods in order to live comfortably, and I am not referring to items purchased for nourishment or necessary for survival. I am talking about the discretionary items we want to possess, as opposed to the necessary items that we need to possess. The amount of goods we consume, and the type and quality of those goods can make a big difference to our net worth. For the purposes of this book, let us call items that do not maintain their value, or lose value over time, and have no resale value, as Type L (L for liability) consumables. Items that maintain a high percentage of their resale value, we will call Type A (A for asset) consumables. Neither of the two is considered assets, but Type A consumables will maintain some value over time, so we will call them assets for the purpose of this book, and Type L consumables, we will call liabilities. An example of how to take advantage of this distinction in consumables is to suppose you purchase a home and fill it with cheap furniture; the odds are, over time, that furniture will become worthless. Let us say, however, that instead you buy high-quality furniture or antique furniture; over time, it could maintain a high percentage of its value, or in the case of antique furniture, it may actually increase

in value over time, providing value to you at a later date while still serving the same purpose as the cheap furniture.

6. *Business ventures*: Businesses can be either assets or liabilities. One year, your business venture can be an asset (revenue exceeds your expenses), the next year it can be a liability (expenses exceed your revenue). There is also the strange example of how a business venture that portrays a liability on paper can be an asset for tax purposes (sole shareholder s-corporation). See Chapter 11, section on profit management.

7. *Houses*: A house can be either a fixed asset or a liability. Learn to buy your homes wisely. Refer to Chapter 6 (Focus on Investing, not on Consuming) on investing in real estate for an example of how a house, if bought wisely, can be an asset. Conversely, if you buy the nicest, most expensive, house in the neighborhood or spend more on your house than it is worth, based on the current real estate market or comparable sales figures, it will be considered a liability.

8. *Cars*: A car can be either a fixed asset or a liability. I recommend buying your car and keeping it for the long term, a minimum of six years. Refer to Chapter 6 (Focus on Investing, not on Consuming) in the section that discusses Earner B for an example of how your car can be an asset and how if you purchase your car and keep it for at least six years, that can lead to savings that will allow you to accumulate more assets. Conversely, if you lease your car or buy a new car every three years, your car will be considered a liability.

9. *Collectibles*: Collectibles, by definition, are assets. Items that increase in value over time. Items such as precious stones, antiques, art, precious metals, and so on. These items are typically purchased and kept for their long-term appreciation potential.

10. *Yourself*: Based on how you act, you can be either an asset or a liability to yourself, your growth potential, and to your company. You represent and are the personification of your company's brand. You need to do everything in your power to continue to learn and better yourself to enhance your brands' image. See Chapter 12 on create and cultivate your brand.

11. *Your relationships*: Similarly, the people who you surround yourself with can be either assets or liabilities to your growth potential and

well-being. You want to accumulate friends, associates, and business partners who can be considered assets. When you embark on the challenge of entrepreneurship, you will encounter many hurdles and obstacles that will require support from not only your family but also from your friends, associates, and business partners. A friend, associate, or business partner who exudes negativity and does not support or believe in you is a liability. On the contrary, one who offers positive support and constructive advice is an asset. Learn to identify which of your friends, associates, or business partners you can classify in the asset column or category and accumulate as many of those as you can and reduce, as much as you can, the ones you would categorize in the liability column.

We, as a society, are accustomed, trained, and judged based on how much stuff we accumulate. How nice our stuff is compared to the stuff of others. We are bombarded with constant advertisement designed to entice us to consume more and more. It is easy to fall into the trap of overconsumption. I would advise, however, that it is okay to consume items for pleasure, but find creative ways to do so, and do so by consuming items that are considered assets such as those listed earlier (art work, collectibles, fine jewelry, and so on). The problem is that most of the stuff we consume are liabilities that do not increase our net worth, but instead they increase the net worth of others. Before you purchase a product, other than the obvious daily required consumables, ask yourself the question: Is this an asset? If the answer is no, ask yourself: Is there a comparable alternative to this product that is, or can eventually be, considered an asset? Entrepreneurs, almost always, make the wise choice.

Another item to consider, which is one of my pet peeves, is the idea of renting or leasing versus buying or owning. I hate to rent or lease. Sometimes, you cannot avoid it, but if you can, never rent but instead buy and own. When you rent or lease, you are making someone else's entrepreneurial dreams come true at the expense of, or to the detriment of, your own. You are accumulating liabilities, not assets. Absent a tax write-off for a business; buying is the way to go, and that holds true for property as well as vehicles, in my opinion.

One final piece of advice on why it is extremely important and beneficial to accumulate assets and reduce liabilities is to use them as a safeguard
or safety net for any unexpected hardships or as mitigation from potential
injury as a result due to undertaking risk. I discussed such a situation in
my life, in Chapter 5 "Do Not Be Afraid to Take Risks" in the section on
how the accumulation of assets can serve to mitigate risk and how it came
in very handy for me in my life. It is a lesson that I cannot stress often
enough as a way to have a backup plan and safety net for troubled times
that can also serve to increase your net worth over time. So, remember,
accumulate assets, not liabilities inclusive of the tangible and intangible
variety.

Chapter 7: Accumulate Assets, Not Liabilities

Recommended Activities

1. Write down a list of all your assets, and break them down into fixed and liquid (A).
2. Write down a list of all your liabilities (L).
3. Find out what you net worth is (A minus L)
4. Create a spreadsheet of your net worth that lists all your assets and liabilities as well as your expenses.
5. Create a budget that meets your needs and see how much is leftover to accumulate more assets.
6. Make a list of all anticipated major expenses in your near future and identify any available alternative options that can provide more or better appreciation or value in the long run and consider your options.

CHAPTER 8

Specialize and Become an Expert

Being unique and setting your own path in life and in business leads to unparalleled experience and expertise worthy of an entrepreneur.

This chapter will focus on helping you identify the area of specialty best suited for you and becoming the best at what you do. We have all heard the saying, it is better to be a big fish in a small pond than a small fish in a big pond. That is the essence of finding a specialty or niche for your business. School will only teach us the very basics and general aspects of our chosen profession, and we all get, for the most part, the same experience and exposure to the craft. By focusing and channeling your energy on a specific aspect of or specialty within your chosen profession, you can more readily develop a more profound understanding of the intricacies involved. You can become an expert. You do not want to be a jack of all trades, but master of none. You want to find a need, within your chosen field, that is neglected or misunderstood that has potential if given the proper attention.

Becoming an expert will set you apart in your field and from your competition. It will allow you the opportunity to create a name and identity for yourself and provide credibility. There are clear-cut ways to become an expert. Next, you will find the eight steps that you need to take to become an expert:

The eight steps to becoming an expert	
1	Gain valuable knowledge and experience
2	Identify an area of specialty
3	Find a mentor
4	Follow the experience, not the money
5	Never stop learning
6	Collaborate
7	Innovate
8	Surround yourself with successful people

1. *Gain valuable knowledge and experience*: There is no better investment than doing whatever it takes to gain valuable knowledge and
experience. The best vehicle for you to obtain knowledge is through
your schooling. The best vehicle for you to obtain experience is
through your job. The best vehicle for you to obtain both is through
accumulated work experience. However, neither your school nor
your job will provide you the full breadth of knowledge and experience that you need to become an entrepreneur and achieve success.
You must supplement those two vehicles with outside knowledge
and experience. You can supplement your knowledge through reading, training, certifications, mentors, and continuing education. You
can supplement your experience through internships, volunteering,
personal association, and changing jobs. Good areas to focus on
to obtain additional knowledge and experience include communications, marketing, accounting, legal and taxation, and investing.
Another particularly important self-investment strategy is to attain
specialized skills. Skills include technical and soft skills. Technical
skills include anything that can help you directly in your profession.
Soft skills include anything that can help you achieve success. In my
case, I gained most of my knowledge through accumulated work
experience. I had the luxury of working for a boss who, for whatever reason, valued versatility and exposed me to all facets of business at an early stage in my career. Knowledge and experience that
included accounting, tax preparation, communications, and marketing. However, I did heavily supplement my soft skill knowledge
through reading and volunteering. I sharpened my technical skills

through research, serving as a peer reviewer, performing forensic investigations, and staying up to date with the latest code changes. I sharpened my soft skills through volunteering, writing, and public speaking.

2. *Identify an area of specialty*: In order to start your career off right, with entrepreneurship in mind, you need to begin to identify potential specialty or niche practice areas in your specific field of practice. A niche can be established in any profession, but it should be in an industry in which you have experience or connections in. Experience and connections from which you can attain specialized knowledge and learn to provide a useful and needed service. The areas that you identify in this chapter will be the foundation for your future business venture. In my case, the specialty fell into my lap, but I was able to recognize the opportunity and take advantage. I was able to see the advantages of working for a small niche firm, and I soaked up all I could from them. Having a specialty is what insulated me from the Great Recession, and it is what allowed me to start my own firm in such an environment. An environment where people were being let go in great numbers due to the downturn in the economy.

3. *Find a mentor*: Once you have identified your specific area of specialty, you need to find out who is the best in that field. Reach out to them, emulate, and learn from them. Some of the biggest entrepreneurs started out working for a pioneer in their field, and after some time, they found a way to improve on the product or services and then went out on their own, sometimes even surpassing their mentor's accomplishments. In my case, my very first mentor was my father. He taught me by example. My next mentor was my first boss at the engineering firm who confided in me enough to allow me to innovate and gave me ever-increasing responsibility in the management side of the engineering business. The third mentor was a building official who was known for his strictness and demanding style. I learned much from each one and would not be where I am today if not for each one of them.

4. *Follow the experience, not the money*: If you want to be an entrepreneur, experience is more valuable than money. Find a mentor or company that will provide you with opportunity for growth, mento-

ring, continuing education, resources, and increasing responsibility. In my case, I stayed at my first engineering job, for over 13 years, despite the poor pay, because of the learning potential and experiences. Money comes and goes. Experience stays with you. I believe there is no such thing as a wasted experience if you learn from it. It provides you with context and teaches you what to do, or not do, when faced with a similar situation in the future. After all, who we are is the sum of our experiences.

5. *Never stop learning*: No one knows everything, and there is always going to be someone hungrier than you, right behind you, or beside you, looking to take your place in line if you stop growing and become complacent. Attend conferences, lectures, read up on new codes, technology, and trends. The moment you stop learning is the moment the synapses and connections between your brain cells start dying. In my case, I enjoy learning something new. I am a fanatic of the human brain and the universe. It is said that when you learn something new, your brain develops new synapses and connections. The brain after all is a muscle, and if you exercise it, it will strengthen. My passion for learning does not stop with learning about business; it continues into wanting to learn about history, the great minds of the past, the new discoveries in science and technology. I believe knowledge is power, and learning provides knowledge, which leads to power. Power in the sense of an engine that propels you forward. Do not ever stagnate; do not ever stop learning. As I said, the moment you stop learning is the moment your brain starts dying. A word of caution, however, when I communicate with young ambitious students about higher education (should they pursue a Master's and/or PhD after graduation or enter the work force?), my advice to them is: It depends...BUT...It does not matter how you acquire knowledge, just that you do. Some of our greatest minds did not have a formal education; hence, what matters is what you do with the acquired and accumulated knowledge. I always add that I am never opposed to higher education and learning, just not at the detriment of experience and practice.

6. *Collaborate*: Learn not only from your mentor, but also from you peers and even from your competition. See what others are doing in

your field. Network and find opportunities to work together with colleagues for mutual benefit. Sometimes, you can be stuck on a certain task, and a discussion with like-minded individuals can trigger an idea. In my case, I have always tried to find common interests with collogues to unite for the betterment of our profession. To see how we can help each other and raise awareness of issues we have in common. Instances of collaboration include discussing code changes, presenting at, and attending colleagues presentations at conferences, performing peer reviews, even working together on projects.

7. *Innovate*: You do not need to try and reinvent the wheel. Identify a product or service that you feel, after thought and research, you can improve on. Find a better way of providing that product or service, faster, better, or cheaper. Focus on improvement of products, services, or processes. In my case, I have been able to streamline the process by which I perform certain tasks and have been able to train my staff to perform those same tasks in the same way, as to be more efficient. It reminds of the story behind the original creators of the McDonald's fast-food preparation procedures. They were able to design a layout, timing, and sequence that maximized productivity. In order to stay ahead of the crowd, you must learn to innovate.

8. *Surround yourself with successful people*: You need to build a good network of other experts who you can share ideas and opportunities with. You should never be the smartest person in the room. Consider yourself, as described in Chapter 6, as the ugliest house in the nicest neighborhood. You want to have room to grow within your surroundings and aspire to be like your neighbors. You want to build your mental equity and increase your self-worth by association, through gradual self-investment and self-improvement. In my case, whenever I found the need for an accountant, a realtor, a lawyer, and such, I always picked their brains and absorbed as much as I could. I am rarely satisfied by being told this is how it is. I will always read up more on the topic and come back with more questions. You will need a good group of advisors who know more than you do in other aspects that involve your profession to fill in the gaps of knowledge necessary to achieve success. Think of it as a battery that naturally

flows from high potential to low potential. If you are always the high potential, you will always be draining and providing the flow of current (ideas) out of you and into someone else. By contrast, if you are always the low potential, you will always be filling and receiving the flow of current (ideas) and charging your brain with every experience and interaction. Surrounding yourself with successful people will expose you to their habits, their way of looking at things, their choice in advisors and investments. It will ultimately provide you with a target to shoot for, a goal, an aspiration.

Because I come from an engineering background and most of my experiences come from being a business founder, owner, and entrepreneur in the engineering profession, I do not consider myself qualified to speak on the specifics of the other professions. Even though all the concepts in this book transcend all professions, I wanted to provide you with a broad perspective. That is why, I have reached out to and interviewed successful entrepreneurs in 12 different professions and sought their opinion and advice so that I could relay it to you. Included in those 12 professions are two atypical professions, politics and philanthropy, both of which I feel can stem from any of the other professions and add a different perspective. I have also included a 13th piece from the perspective of an often forgotten individual in most entrepreneurial stories, the spouse or significant other, that quite often stands silently behind the entrepreneur, but most always plays an integral part in the story. I have carefully chosen these individuals not only because of their success, they are all successful, but for how they were able to take advantage of a unique specialty in their field or how they have demonstrated their passion and commitment and embody the qualities that fit the mold of a true entrepreneur. I have purposefully selected individuals who provide a wide range of backgrounds, including: medicine, law, engineering, architecture, accounting, business, construction, media relations, real estate, photography, politics, and philanthropy. I have asked my wife, Frances, to write a piece from the perspective of the significant other.

The way I went about it is that I submitted a list of four questions for them to answer (the 10 typical professions), and after I reviewed the answers, I communicated with them to try and draw up their unique story in order to create a narrative that would provide you with the best possible advice. I then asked different and more appropriate questions to the two atypical professions (politics and philanthropy) as well as for the significant other, to round out the chapter. What I found out after putting together their stories has validated what is written in this book. I am extremely appreciative to each one of them for their time and effort. The questions were:

1. How did you achieve your goal of becoming an entrepreneur?
2. What advice would you give an aspiring entrepreneur in your profession?
3. What areas and opportunities of innovation do you see for your profession in general?
4. What is the best way to become an expert in your field?

What follows is a series of unique stories and advice from a broad spectrum of professions and personalities with wide-ranging levels of success, all of which embody what it means to be an entrepreneur. I hope you enjoy reading their stories as much as I enjoyed writing them.

1. Medicine

Entrepreneur: Dr. Flor A. Mayoral
Company: Mayoral Dermatology
Specialty: Dermatology

Success happens when you are passionate, and you show up—consistently—without questioning how much effort or time it will take for you to get there.

—Dr. Flor A. Mayoral

Flor is a dermatologist. She embodies the meaning of true entrepreneurship. She started with nothing, followed her dreams, made sacrifices, took risks, found a specialty, founded her own firm, innovated, made a name for herself, became an expert, and created a legacy for her two daughters, who work side by side with her at her company. In the true spirit of entrepreneurship, she has passions outside of her business, shares her knowledge, and gives back to the community. She is an avid and accomplished photographer and a constant on the media circuit.

Flor was born in 1955 in Cuba to a family of bakers who emigrated to Miami in 1967. She is the oldest of three children. Her two siblings are Osvaldo Mayoral, a dentist, and Ana Margarita Mayoral, who ran La Rosa Bakery with her parents in Miami, FL, until she passed away from cancer in 2015. Her parents, Osvaldo and Mercedes Mayoral, are currently 92 and 85 years old, respectively, and continue to work every day. They always encouraged her to get an education. She has three children: a son, Andy, who is a CPA turned chef, and two daughters, Janelle Vega and Adriane Pompa, who both became dermatologists and practice side by side with her. She attended the University of Florida and earned a bachelor's degree in pharmacology in 1976 and a medical degree in 1981. She did her postgraduate training at the University of Miami and specialized in dermatology. Flor started her practice about 35 years ago when she finished her residency as a dermatologist and cutaneous surgeon. Over the years, it has evolved into a practice that specializes is cosmetic procedures—for face and body. They are known for radiofrequency (RF) treatments for rejuvenation and currently have seven RF devices in the office. They are currently in the midst of performing three clinical studies: one with an existing filler and two with neurotoxins: a Phase 3 trial of a new product and a toxin dosing study. Flor's accomplishments and contributions to her profession, over the past 35 years, are almost too many to mention. Some of the more notable ones include: working with numerous companies to evaluate their devices to help elucidate a better protocol for their use, lecturing on RF and fillers (both domestically and abroad), teaching her colleagues (both domestically and abroad) on injection techniques, serving as an adjunct professor at the Miller School of Medicine's Department of Dermatology (includes having visiting fellows, dermatologists, regularly visit her practice from all over the world), mentoring dermatologists (both domestically and abroad), volunteering as faculty member at the Jackson Memorial Hospital clinics, writing peer-reviewed articles and lecturing at meetings (both domestically and abroad), and serving on the Advisory Panel of Dermatologists for the Consumer Products Division of L'Oreal Paris, USA. Flor's community involvement is notable and includes involvement and support of Urban Promise Miami (UPM) since 2010. UPM is a nonprofit organization started by her niece, Judge Kristy Nuñez, and her childhood friend Dr. Ana Ojeda, a psychologist. Their mission is to keep at-risk children off the streets by providing free after-school programs and summer camps. Their headquarters is located in Little Havana, Fl. Flor supports Bridge to Hope, on an annual basis, a nonprofit organization that helps families in crisis. Flor has also served on an advisory board for Florida International University's Frost Museum for two years. She sits on the Board of Directors of the Coral Gables Art Cinema and of DORCAM (Doral Contemporary Art Museum), a nonprofit organization, where she, at times, helps to organize several exhibitions, free to the public.

Flor never really had the goal of becoming an entrepreneur, but she knew that she wanted to become successful in her field. She believes "Success happens when you are passionate, and you show up—consistently—without questioning how much effort or time it will take for you to get there." She found herself, as a young dermatologist, in private practice and without the financial means to purchase a hair removal laser. She started renting lasers from a company once a week at the rate of 1,000 U.S. dollars for a half day, which included two to three lasers. She had trouble making the effort worthwhile due to canceled appointments or patients coming in with tans that made them ineligible for treatment. Therefore, she decided to buy one for herself. That decision made all the difference in the world. She now has 16 lasers in her office, and she has not looked back since.

The advice she would give an aspiring entrepreneur in her field is "perseverance and hard work are more likely to make you successful than intelligence or luck," "never be afraid of change," "solve problems, don't create them." She goes on to add "my goal has always been to treat patients like I would like to be treated (with respect and kindness) and to offer them the latest innovations in the field of dermatology." She believes strongly that you should surround yourself with people who are happy and share your goals and to never be afraid to remove an employee who is unkind to a patient or co-worker. Her final piece of advice is to share your success with your employees by rewarding their performance.

Flor believes the areas of opportunities and innovation lie in the fields of body and facial contouring, fillers, skin tightening, fat removal, cosmeceuticals, lectures, clinical studies, and mentoring. She believes the field of dermatology "has evolved into a vibrant and ever-changing field with innovations at every turn."

Flor believes that the best way to become an expert in her field is "if you find something you excel at within your field, align your practice goals so that you have the opportunity to perform the procedure more often. This will make you an expert in a specific area of your chosen profession, giving you greater credibility and a large pool of patients will seek your knowledge and advice." She believes you should create your own "before and after" photos of the procedures you perform. She advises to become a trainer to your colleagues in techniques that you excel at and lecture at national or local dermatologic society meetings as well as to participate in skin cancer screenings at your local hospital. She advises that you should let people know who you are by displaying your diplomas prominently in a public area of your office. She advises to "say yes to every radio or TV speaking engagement—even if you hate getting up early in the morning and driving across town." She says, "people think you know more when you are on TV." She advises however, to take some media training courses before embarking on the sharing of your knowledge on a public platform. She says, doing so "will teach you to stay on message, to be concise, and to deliver key phrases…." She also advocates to be active on social media, which "offers unending opportunities to reach out to an even greater audience." She continues to say, "make sure every accomplishment worthy of announcing is put on social media." She concludes "now a days, if it's not on social media—it didn't happen…"

2. Law

Entrepreneur: Anthony M. Lopez
Company: Marin, Eljaiek, Lopez & Martinez. P.L. d/b/a Your Insurance Attorney ™
Specialty: Plaintiff's insurance litigation

> *As the owner of my own law firm my revenue is never capped by a function of time, but rather on the amount of business I can generate, and the results obtained from that business.*
>
> —Anthony M. Lopez

Anthony is an attorney specializing in plaintiff's insurance litigation. He exemplifies what it means to find a specialty, work smart, and become the best. His passion for his work and his clients shines clearly through his personality. He has built an identity and name for himself in his field and is ever present on social media and TV. Not only is he a successful attorney, he is also an accomplished pilot.

Anthony was born in Miami, FL. He is married to his wife, Dr. Nicole Martin, and has a newly born son named Greyson. He came from humble beginnings. He was raised by a single working mother who did everything in her power to provide for him and his sister, Marilyn. He put himself through college and law school, earning a bachelor's in business information systems from Florida International University and graduating from St. Thomas University School of Law while working full time. He now owns one of Florida's largest plaintiff insurance litigation law firms with revenue exceeding 20-million U.S. dollars. Anthony started his law firm in 2006 with five people, which has grown to over 120 employees and occupies 30,000 sq. ft. of office space. Anthony's firm has success-fully tried insurance cases all over the State of Florida, and they pride themselves on achieving a consistent winning record. His firm is actively involved with Kristi House Children's Advocacy Center, a not-for-profit committed to protecting and safeguarding abused children.

Anthony never set out to be an entrepreneur. He says it was "a func-tion of circumstance and analyzing time versus money." He realized and stated that "working for someone else capped my ability to generate money while still working the same amount of time" He adds "As the owner of my own law firm my revenue is never capped by a function of time, but rather on the amount of business I can generate, and the results obtained from that business."

The advice he would give an aspiring entrepreneur in his field is "Do not chase money. Chase an area of the law that you are passionate about and the money will follow." Anthony believes that aspiring entrepreneurs should "focus on practicing in an area of the law that makes you excited to get out of bed in the morning and go to work." He adds "I am passionate about helping people [to] not get taken advantage of by big business. The old adage of David versus Goliath has always inspired me." He contin-ues by saying "this is what drove me to representing people against their insurance companies. The insurance industry is built on huge companies trying to take advantage of the little [people] by not paying valid claims and forcing [the] policyholder to either fight or walk away with nothing." He concludes by saying "I like the fact that I don't make a dollar unless I win the case. My clients and I are aligned from the outset with one goal, to win."

Anthony believes the areas of opportunities and innovation in the law lie in the taking advantage of technology. He states that "one of the reasons that my law firm is successful is because we innovate. The land-scape for generating business in the law industry has changed immensely over the last decade and technology plays an integral part in how we generate clients." He adds "we leverage social media, television, YouTube and many other creative mediums to bring in business." He goes on to add that "Every area of the law has the potential to be specialized in and focused on. I truly believe that if you focus on one particular area of the law that you love, and hone your skills in that particular area to be the best, you will find success, or rather, it will find you."

Anthony believes that the best way to become an expert in his field is through "experience and constantly trying cases." He also adds that "No matter what you do in life you will find essentially two types of people: leaders and followers." He states that "If you want to build a name for yourself you have to lead the pack and the best way to do this is to be the best or create a new way of doing things." He continues by saying "If you are content on working the same way as everyone else you better be content with a mediocre career." He advises to "Wake up early and go to bed late studying and spend the waking hours honing your craft. Take on the tough cases that no one wants and figure out a way to win for your clients." He concludes his advice by saying "Do not become complacent with each success. Keep at it. Trail blazers are remembered because they took a chance where no one else would or thought to take a chance."

3. Engineering

Entrepreneur: Anthony Fasano, P.E.
Company: Engineering Management Institute
Specialty: Executive coach and trainer for engineers and technical professionals

> *The best way to be an expert is to pick a topic, focus on it, learn every-thing about it, practice it, then once you've done that, write and speak on it as much as you can.*
>
> —Anthony Fasano, P.E.

Anthony is a licensed professional engineer who practiced civil engineer-ing. He has a passion for and excels at the soft skills required to be suc-cessful when working in a professional engineering environment. He had that entrepreneurial spirit and mindset early on in his career. He has man-aged, despite negative feedback from peers, to channel that passion into creating a niche focused on helping engineers become better managers and leaders. He planned to do this by building an executive coaching and training firm for engineers, even though many felt there was no demand. To date, EMI is one of the go-to training organizations for engineers worldwide, and Anthony continues to be passionate about helping engineers and technical professionals obtain the tools necessary for success.

Anthony was born in 1978 in Suffern, New York, a suburb of New York City. He has two younger brothers Christopher and Michael. He is married to his wife, Jill, who is also a civil engineer, and they have three kids, Brianna, AJ, and Penelope. He earned his Bachelor of Science degree in Civil and Environmental Engineering from Lafayette College and his Master of Science degree in Civil Engineering from Columbia University. He started working as a civil engineering in 2000. In 2013, Anthony decided to start his first podcast to help grow his coaching and training company for engineers. People told him engineers would never listen to a career-related podcast. Four years later, that podcast, The Engineering Career Coach, has been downloaded over 2 million times and was cited by Forbes as one of the top 15 most inspiring for professionals in 2017. Today, Anthony is building the Engineering Management Institute, a global coaching and training firm that helps engineering companies develop leaders. Anthony has gone on to start and grow five niche podcasts, including The Italian American Podcast (which has featured guests like Mike Piazza and Franco Harris) and helped him to find living relatives in Italy. He has also sold a podcast for six figures to a biotech company. He is the author of several books including *Engineer Your Own Success: 7 Key Elements to Creating and Extraordinary Engineering Career* and *The Content Marketing Equation: Start or Grow Your Online Business Using the Power of Blogging Podcasting and Content Creation*. Fasano has also coauthored a series of children's books with his 11-year-old daughter titled *Purpee the Purple Dragon*. They have delivered hundreds of books to pediatric cancer centers around the world. He also speaks regularly at elementary schools on the subject of engineering.

Anthony became an entrepreneur after he practiced as an engineer for some time and realized that "successful engineers have great soft skills, they can communicate they can network, they can delegate effectively." Once he decided to develop those skills for himself, his career took off, and he was promoted and asked to train other engineers at his firm on these skill sets. That is when he realized that this was a major problem in engineering. He figured, if there were so many people in his company who struggled with these soft skills, how much demand and need must there be across the country for training engineers to develop these skills? That is when he decided to get his coaching certificate, go through the training, quit his job, a safe job with a good salary, and build his firm and travel the county with the purpose of helping engineers become leaders. He has been doing that ever since. He advises that, "You have to find a need that's out there, that matches something that you're good at, where you can deliver value, and then put the two together."

The advice he would give an aspiring entrepreneur in engineering is that, "You have to go into any profession or any business venture under the approach or perspective or mindset of *it's going to be a long haul, it's going to be a long run and you need to do the fundamental things right consistently every day to build a business and to bring a vision to reality.*" He goes on to say that, "Entrepreneurship, while it has it's exciting moments, also has moments that are monotonous, you have to constantly and consistently make sales calls, deliver your services at high quality, and have processes and systems in place in your business to ensure quality control to make sure you are meeting your clients expectations." He concludes that, "It's all about fundamentals and being consistent, and if you do that, you will be setting yourself up for success."

Anthony believes the areas of opportunities and innovation in engineering, more specifically, the coaching and training aspect of engineering, lie in doing "a better job of creating training that transfers...how do training participants actually transfer the lessons learned back to the job?" Especially when one has a very hectic work schedule. At his current firm, Engineering Management Institute, he has developed techniques to do this by creating frameworks in the training and by giving the trainees small assignments and sending them reinforcement videos to drive the information into the psyche. Otherwise he says, people will participate in the training sessions, but not actually retain anything.

Anthony believes that the best way to become an expert is to, "Pick a topic in your field where there is opportunity and focus on it, but you first need to understand and practice it. You then need to write and speak to build your expertise." He advises to write articles, speak at conferences, and perform interviews related to the subject matter. He summarizes that,

"The best way to be an expert is to pick a topic, focus on it, learn everything about it, practice it, then once you've done that, write and speak on it as much as you can."

4. Architecture

Entrepreneur: Daphne Gurri
Company: Gurri Matute, PA
Specialty: Aviation, education, civic and federal, and health care design

Find out what your true passion is and why you are doing what you are doing. Answering that question will make it easier for people to follow your vision and that includes potential clients, and employees.

—Daphne Gurri

Daphne is an award-winning architect who was born to lead. She has always had the entrepreneurial spirit and passion. Although the reason for starting her firm was to be able to see her own unique designs being constructed, over the years, Daphne has evolved to love being an entrepreneur as much as being an architect.

Daphne was born in Corpus Christi, Texas, and is married to her husband, Jose. They have 3 children—Isabella (25), Ignacio (23), and Eva (14). Her family moved to Miami when she was only three months old, where they have lived ever since. Even while she was in middle school, Daphne's first passion was ballet, followed closely by painting, drawing, ceramics, and weaving. While studying in Miami Dade College as a freshman student, she changed her major from art to architecture, still unsure that this path was the right one. She ultimately earned a Bachelor of Architecture from the University of Miami in 1988 and a Master of Science and Advanced Architectural Design from Columbia University in 1992. Following the recession in the early 1990s and inconsistent job opportunities, she decided to open her own private practice as a sole proprietor—Daphne I Gurri, AIA. Her husband, Jose G Matute, also an architect, joined the firm in 1999, which prompted the firm's name change to Gurri Matute PA. They have had their private practice for 24 years, which specializes in the areas of aviation, education, civic or federal, and health care projects. Some of her accomplishments include being awarded "Young Architect of the Year" in 2000 by the Miami Chapter of the American Institute of Architects, "Best Overall Architectural Design for a Custom Residence" in 2008 from the Builders Association of South Florida, and "Outstanding Achievement as a Woman-Owned Business and Overall Civic and Community Involvement" in 2012 by Women Extraordinaire, to name a few. Daphne is also highly active in the community. Currently, she is the 2020 President of the Miami Chapter of the American Institute of Architects and past Post-President to the South Florida's Post for the Society of American Military Engineers. She was the founder of STEAM Speaks, a program she created over five years ago to encourage young students to explore career paths in architecture, engineering, and construction using Minecraft and Legos.

Daphne has never been a follower. As she puts it, "some of us feel that we do not belong in a place, whether it is in a corporate world or if it's following directions from others." She goes on the say that "some of us feel compelled to lead and usually those people possess the characteristics needed to be an entrepreneur. Those characteristics often include being a risk-tasker, having a strong will, making bold decisions, and following his/her heart." She concludes by saying that "building a business from scratch is an extremely bold decision and takes a lot of persistence and courage. I can say I used those attributes to build my business." Many of the challenges that she faced while starting her firm in 1996 were, as she puts it, "the lack of steady income, lack of clients, lack of business knowledge and lack of time to both design and at the same time, be an effective business owner." She goes on to add "One strategy that I implemented was simultaneously serving as an Adjunct Professor of architectural design at Florida International University School of Architecture which I did over 8 years to not only have additional income for my family, but also to stay engaged in architectural design by teaching others." She admits that "the lack of business knowledge was a critical setback as an entrepreneur." Another strategy she did to overcome her lack of knowledge in accounting was to take business classes at Miami Dade College after she had already been practicing for more than 15 years. She states that "The added knowledge I received from this, and my drive to succeed, have been the reason why I have succeeded in growing my firm from a one person office to a mid-sized firm with 15 employees." However, as she recounts, "my love of being an entrepreneur was not immediate and was accompanied by many obstacles and challenges in a field that is highly competitive and realizes fairly thin profits even during a good economy."

The advice she would give an aspiring entrepreneur in her field is to "find out what your true passion is and the why you are doing what you are doing." She says that "answering that question will make it easier for people to follow your vision and that includes potential clients, and employees." She adds that "aside from that, in order to be successful as an entrepreneur you need to have good finances…" She continues by saying that "in order to start a business, it is really advisable that you have a business plan and some capital. I will say to save up at least a year's worth of salaries and living expenses for yourself." Speaking from personal experience, she estimates that "it will take at least two years or maybe even longer for a startup business to start generating a stable income." She emphasizes that "this is especially true when you are in a field that offers Architecture/Engineering/construction services which are based on a per project basis, unlike accountants who receive recurring income year after year from their clients." She concludes by saying that "another alternative is to seek some kind of a recurring income that provides a steady monthly income to the business, sometimes it is a little hard to get but it sure helps paying the bills."

Daphne believes the areas of opportunities and innovation in architecture, engineering, and construction, "lie in the use of robotics in accelerating the process of how we build." She adds, "I think this is one of the areas where our industry really falls behind. We are still building one area at a time, and one element at a time, and I think that the area of robotics and advanced software will help accelerate that process."

Daphne believes that if you want to become an expert in the field of architecture "you really need to make a mark for yourself." She adds that "It is also important to have some kind of specialization." She goes on to advise that "if you are becoming an Architect, pick an area that you really enjoy working in whether that is healthcare or historic preservation work … and so on. Once you find your niche, become an expert in that area." She adds "the second thing will be branding. Branding can be best described as how people see and talk about you. It is important to pay attention to the quality of your work, and the promises to your client/customer." She concludes by saying that "an effective brand strategy gives you a major edge in increasingly competitive markets."

5. Accounting

Entrepreneur: Philip Shechter
Company: Shechter & Associates
Specialty: CPA and forensic accounting

> *Learn everything you can from those training you. Be a sponge. Don't say no to any assignment regardless of whether you see a future in the work being assigned. Be courteous, smart, and responsive and wait for your door to open. It will open and you will find your path.*
> —Philip Shechter

Philip is a forensic accountant specializing in litigation advisory services. He is a tireless worker with an impeccable work ethic and is extremely dedicated to his craft. He learned his work ethic from his father and has tried to pass it along to his kids. Philip has paid his dues, worked hard, and has reaped the rewards of his hard work and dedication through entrepreneurship.

Philip was born in Miami, Florida. He has four children. A daughter named Jennifer, a CPA and partner in his firm; a son named Matthew, who works with him and Jennifer; Jesse, a doctor, who is a resident working in a Hospital associated with Harvard University; and his youngest son, Kevin, who is graduating Eckerd college with a bachelor's in business and is soon to join the family CPA business. Philip attended the University of Florida where he earned a Bachelor of Science Degree in accounting in 1982. Philip began working with his father, who had a small CPA firm on Miami Beach, three days after he graduated from college. In those days, CPA firms did everything, so he was originally trained in tax, audits, bookkeeping, and accounting. Philip became a partner at his father's firm eight years after he started working for him. The firm added partners and merged throughout the years. In 2018, Philip finally decided to create his own firm with his daughter and has added his two sons to the family business. He has 38 years of experience in audit, tax consulting, litigation support, and business valuation services. Philip and his daughter and sons offer traditional accounting and tax services at Shechter & Associates, LLP. Philip also oversees the firm's litigation support business and business valuation services through an affiliated firm, Shechter & Everett, LLP, where he and Michael Everett practice. Philip and Michael have practiced together providing litigation support services for over 20 years. Philip has been involved with over 8,000 litigation matters, has been qualified as an expert, and has provided expert testimony more than 2,000 times in state and federal courts related to commercial litigation and family law engagements. He also serves as a *neutral CPA* or mediator in divorce matters. His groundbreaking work in this area has been documented in the AICPA's *Journal of Accountancy*. Philip was recognized as one of the "Top CPA's and Financial Professionals" by the South Florida Legal Guide from 2005 to 2019. His firm provides pro bono services to protect the rights of mothers and fathers and their children.

Philip was destined to be an entrepreneur. He quips that "I was an entrepreneur when I was first born." He explains that his dad was a CPA and an entrepreneur. His first exposure to entrepreneurship was growing up watching his dad, as he puts it, "meet clients, sell to clients, market to clients, gain friends, market to friends, making friends become clients, making clients become friends." It was that hands-on training with his father that prepared him for entrepreneurship at a young age. He has attempted to transfer that same mindset to his kids. He goes on to add that "my daughter and sons are working with me and I am hoping the same training will work for them." However, he cautions that "millennials are much harder to train than baby boomers or traditionalists," and he advises that it "just takes more time for them to accept anything told to them by a baby boomer unless they can read it on the Internet." He jokes that "sometimes I feel like posting things on the Internet and then finding a way for the millennials I am training to read it."

The advice he would give an aspiring entrepreneur in his field is "you have to pay the dues. There is no easy way to get the experience in this industry," and "you have to be at the right place and the right time." He tells his story of how he happened upon his now specialty of litigation support expert as such "I had no idea I would become a litigation support expert. Over 25 years ago a client going through a divorce asked me for assistance and before I knew it, I had testified over 2,000 times and handled over 8,000 cases." He goes on to say that "the litigation practice is over a 5 million dollar a year practice." He continues his advice to aspiring entrepreneurs by stressing to them to "learn everything you can from those training you. Be a sponge. Don't say no to any assignment regardless of whether you see a future in the work being assigned. Be courteous, smart, and responsive and wait for your door to open. It will open and you will find your path." He concludes by adding "you don't need to start out with a path. You should just start out learning, being friendly, supportive and the door will magically open. It might take a day, a year, 10 years… but your door will open, and you will figure out your path."

Philip believes the areas of opportunities and innovation lie in changing with the times and specializing. He believes that the CPA profession is changing and goes on to say that the CPA profession "used to be to help people with their books and records, prepare tax returns and audit financials. Now it is advisory, advisory, advisory." He adds that "computers have eliminated the preparing of books and records. Computers have reduced the complexity of filing tax returns. Computers have made auditing more IT involved, and less people involved." He concludes by saying that "CPAs have now become 'financial advisors', they assist with litigation issues, they assist with selling businesses, buying businesses, tax planning and assisting an owner of a business as to how to run their business more efficiently." He adds that "the role of CPA has changed and will continue to change. It has become highly specialized." He continues to say that "a tax advisor is different than an auditor which is different than a business advisor." He says that "CPAs used to get a BS degree and went out into the world as a generalist. Now a CPA needs a master's degree, at a minimum, then needs to get certifications in an area of specialty and there is no longer the concept of a generalist." Philip believes that technology is the future of the CPAs. As he states it, "all millennials seem to be versed in technology. Having and embracing IT technology is the core training. Once that is accomplished, then advising becomes the key." He says that "in order to be an advisor it takes patience and learning. Learning by finding a mentor and taking their experience and making it become your experience." Philip recounts that "as a young CPA, I would watch my father, listen and absorb the interactions between my father and his clients. Watching and absorbing for years. Then taking that approach and mimicking it and making it my way of dealing with clients." Philip believes this method of learning and training has not changed. As he puts it, "just the tools have changed, and the topics to advise on have moved from compliance-oriented tax and auditing to advising."

Philip believes that the best way to become an expert in his field is "experience, experience, experience." He recommends to "work for someone who is well rounded and handles many different types of forensic accounting assignments." He adds that "the field is very diverse and getting a good background of the types of forensic accounting assignments will allow you to decide what type of forensic accounting you want to do." He continues to say that "forensic accountants need to have a diverse background to be able to testify in court. So, preparing tax returns (working in a tax department) preparing audits (working in an audit department) would provide detailed background to be a better testifying witness."

6. Business

Entrepreneur: Jaime Mitrani
Company: Giardino Salads
Specialty: Casual fast-food industry

> *You will never be great at something you don't love to do, so the only way to do great work is to truly love and enjoy it.*
>
> —Jaime Mitrani

Jaime is a casual fast-food business franchise owner who started his career as an attorney. He was never attracted to the conventional career path nor to the daily grind associated with working for someone else. He figured out, early on, that the right path for him was entrepreneurship, and he managed, during his two years working in law, to accumulate the necessary knowledge and funding to make that dream a reality. He did his research, planned well, and did not wait long for his opportunity. When the right opportunity presented itself, he pounced. He was born to be an entrepreneur.

Jaime was born in Miami, FL. He is married to his wife, Dana, and has two beautiful kids, Lani and Jacob. He studied architecture in high school and thoroughly enjoyed it, but quickly realized that his life as an architect would be *a grind*, so instead, in 2002, he decided to attend the University of Florida and major in business finance with a minor in entrepreneurship for what he thought to be "a quicker and easier path to success with more life freedom." After college, he applied to law school because, as he recalls, "I always said I wanted to be a lawyer," even though he had not ever really experienced the practice of law. In 2006, he attended law school at the University of North Carolina at Chapel Hill. Always with one eye on entrepreneurship, he focused his classes on business law-related topics. As he had felt about the study of architecture, he also felt about the study of law... he thoroughly enjoyed it. However, also like he had felt with his vision of his life as an architect, it was during a summer associate position at a very large international law firm that he soon discovered that the practice of law and his vision of his life as a lawyer would also not provide him the freedom he was seeking. As he put it, "I learned that unlike in business, in law there were no shortcuts or fast passes to success, and long hours and long years would be required." Nonetheless, after law school, he was offered and accepted a position to work as an associate attorney at a law firm. Thus, he would begin his career as an attorney. As fate would have it, due to the market crash in 2008, the position at his firm was deferred for six months. Instead, during the six months when his position was deferred, his firm set him up with a part-time corporate law position at an electronics retailer. This afforded him his first taste of the business world. While there he got to experience the intersect between law and business, he quickly realized that he enjoyed the business side of the practice much more. This revelation notwithstanding, in 2010, when his deferment had ended, he officially began his career as a lawyer in the practice of financial services, international business, health care, and entertainment law. It did not take him long to realized that law was not the field for him; in fact, as he puts it "on my first day after a full day of orientation, I sat on the 33rd floor, in my cushy chair and office with spectacular views ...and realized I needed to start planning my exit from this world." During the next two years, he learned as much as he could about general business, contracts, and corporate law.

He decided to research opportunities in casual fast-food franchises, as he had worked in restaurants in high school and college and had enjoyed the experiences. This is when he discovered a young franchise called Giardino Salads. He had managed to save enough money in the two years working at the law firm and decided to make the leap into franchise ownership. As he recalled, even though the people he worked with were incredible and collegial people "without a full leap of faith (quitting the firm completely), the possibility of still being in that same place for 20 years was scary enough to give me the final push I needed." He quit his job on January 18, 2012, and six months later, along with a partner, he purchased his first Giardino Salads and managed to double sales within the first year. Today, he owns five stores and has acquired an ownership stake in the franchise entity, Giardino Enterprises, along with the founders. His goal is "to grow Giardino Salads into a powerhouse regional franchise." Giardino is an employee-friendly organization that strives to help their employees find success within the organization and on to whatever endeavors or careers they may pursue. Jaime and Giardino are also heavily involved in the South Florida community, including charitable causes like the Live Like Bella foundation and the South Florida chapter of the Cystic Fibrosis foundation. They are also gearing up to become involved with local schools to teach kids about healthy meals and food.

Jaime always knew he wanted to be an entrepreneur; it was in his blood. As he puts it, "ever since I can remember, I have been doing business." As a five-year-old, he would sell baseball cards to the other neighborhood kids, usually for a loss, as he recalls. At age 10, he started a car wash business, and he got his first real job at age 14, mopping dried beer off the floor of a local pub and busing tables. During his years at college, he ran a marketing and promotions company, promoting events, night clubs, venues, and pool parties. He could not wait to leave his job as an attorney at an international law firm, despite the good money and nice office with a great view. As soon as he graduated law school and before he began his career as a lawyer, his mind was already set on entrepreneurship. It was only a matter of how and what to focus on. His goal of becoming an entrepreneur was finally realized in 2012 when, along with a partner, he purchased his first Giardino Salads, a casual fast-food franchise that sells "the best salads, wraps, grain bowls and soups."

The advice he would give an aspiring entrepreneur in his field, starting with those trapped in conventional careers, as he was, is "watch out for jobs that take all of your time for money, in life, time is the most valuable resource we have." He adds that "there is a way out." He goes on to say that "it requires careful thought, planning and attempting to figure out what exactly you want to do with your life before you attempt to change your career path." He cautions "beware 'of' the golden handcuffs: a nice house and a fancy car will not truly make you happy if you don't enjoy your day to day work. It's like riding in a limo to and from prison every day…not worth it." He advises that "there is never the perfect time, so just pick a time and do it and go all in." For entrepreneurs who wish to get in the franchise business, he adds "there are so many franchises out there. Many are fads, and will die within a few years, and they will take your large investment with them. Find a product or food that can withstand the test of time …a concept that is financially sound and provides a great return on investment, and that is simplicity and growth and technologically focused, so that your business can have a 10, 20 or even 30 year run." He concludes that "you will never be great at something you don't love to do, so the only way to do great work is to truly love and enjoy it."

Jaime believes the areas of opportunities and innovation in the franchise business lie in "simple growth." He states "make things easier from an operational standpoint, so that it is easier to grow. Innovation in my type of business is food-related and product related, but innovation also includes the delivery method of that food." He cautions that "dine in and take out are being squeezed by technology and the desire for convenience…growth and adaptation is always needed, and ever evolving, and if you don't evolve with it, you will fall behind."

Jaime believes that the best way to become an expert in his field is to "immerse yourself in what you do, always try to be the best, spend the time, and learn, learn, learn. Always ask questions, find a mentor in your field, read industry publications."

7. Construction

Entrepreneur: James "Jimmy" Tate
Company: Tate Capital Real Estate Solutions
Specialty: Real estate development

> *In order to be successful, you must be clear with your vision. Set your goals both short term and long term. Determine the best path for you, as an individual, to accomplish these goals as all paths are not the same. There are many ways to get to the top of the mountain.*
>
> —James "Jimmy" Tate

Jimmy is a real estate developer, among other things, whose expertise and specialty, as he puts it "is being able to find the common denominator (Basic Business Principles) in all businesses and then ascertain how best to apply those Basic Business Principles to all of our businesses in order to achieve success." He is humble and approachable and has remained deeply passionate, despite his tremendous success.

Jimmy was born and raised in South Florida. He married his wife, Janie, in 1989. They have three daughters named Jordyn, Erin, and Megan. Jimmy earned a degree in Bachelor of Arts in Economics from the University of Florida where he studied real estate analysis, urban economics, public finance, government regulation of business, economic and business statistics, and introduction to engineering. Jimmy has been an integral part of the multifaceted Tate family business for over 30 years. Jimmy cofounded, with his brother Kenny, Tate Development Corporation, which has developed, owned, and managed commercial, industrial, and luxury single- and multi-family properties. Jimmy is also the owner and principal of TKO-Evolution Apparel, a 90-million U.S. dollars a year apparel company that specializes in the manufacturing and importing of primarily men's and women's apparel under private labels for well-known national brands and retailers. Today, his apparel manufacturing firm does approximately (pre-COVID-19) 90 million U.S. dollars at wholesale a year. That equates to well over 200 million U.S. dollars a year at retail. In 2009, Tate Capital was formed for the purpose of acquiring distressed debt opportunities. Jimmy's most recent venture was the acquisition of the Bahia Mar Resort, Hotel and Marina in Fort Lauderdale Beach, Florida. He is in the planning stage of its billion-dollar mixed-use redevelopment effort. They recently obtained a master site plan approval to develop a 1.75-billion U.S. dollars, 40-acre, master planned community, which will consist of approximately 1,000,000 sq. ft. of residential product, 165,000 sq. ft. of commercial and waterfront restaurant space, a 250 mega-yacht marina, a brand new 256-key luxury hotel, a marina village commercial area with retail and food and beverage, a ¾-mile long and 20 ft. wide boardwalk around the marina, and several acres of parks and other amenities throughout. Over the years, the various Tate companies have developed and constructed close to 100 properties, as well as owned, operated, and managed a real estate portfolio well in excess of one billion U.S. dollars. Jimmy has a strong sense of community. He currently serves on the Board of Trustees of the Mount Sinai Medical Center, the Advisory Board of the North Miami Museum of Contemporary Art, and the Development Committee of Miami Country Day School. Over the years, he has also been a member of the Advisory Board of Lehrman Community Day School, the Florida International University Outreach Development Council Board, North Miami Mayor's Economic Task Force Education Committee, Board of Directors for North Miami Museum of Contemporary Art, and President of Westview County Club, to name a few.

James was born to be an entrepreneur. As he states, "I have been blessed with an abundance of success. 1983—While in college at University of Florida, I was working at the Villa Del Ray Golf Course. I realized that the Pro Shop was selling a product that was not easy to get. The name of the product was Lacoste. I also knew that many discount sporting goods stores would love to have access to this product. So, I saw an opportunity in the market whereby I could buy the Lacoste product at wholesale through the Pro Shop's buying office and then I would job (sell) the product all over town. I made approximately $10,000 that summer by doing this." He continues, "1985-1986—I was working for my family's real estate development company learning the development and construction business from my brother Kenny and my father Stanley. One afternoon during lunch, I was cashing my check in a bank called Sunrise Savings and Loan, who were actually banking our development. I was only 23 years old but very curious, very communicative, and very entrepreneurial. I don't recall how or why, but I was in the bank president's office striking up a conversation mainly about how I liked what I was doing, and so on. I explained that I enjoyed learning the business, but my aspirations where much bigger than just continuing down that path working for my brother and father. I explained how I wanted to branch out on my own while I was young and had no real expenses and only my own mouth to feed. During our meeting, he showed me a list of Real Estate Owned (REO) assets that the S&L had taken back through foreclosure. REO's are real estate that the bank takes back from borrowers after they default on their mortgages through a process called foreclosure. In short, I identified 12 partially developed waterfront lots in Jacaranda, Plantation, FL (a high-end luxury master planned community) that I wanted to buy. My entrepreneurial spirit combined with my hunger, passion, and vision allowed me to visualize myself becoming a large developer in time. I met with my brother Kenny and told him that I no longer wanted to work for him and our father. I shared my idea of starting my own real estate business with Kenny, told him that I needed him to help me with the books and controls and that I would handle the construction, marketing and sales. I suggested that he remain with Dad since he was married and had kids at the time and I would head out and take the risk conditioned upon him watching over me from a financial perspective (back office, books and records, etc.). Neither of us had the money required to buy these lots and finish the job, so I asked Kenny to help me create a proforma (budget) and a cash flow analysis that we could present to our father for whom I was prepared to ask to lend us the money to acquire these lots. Our father was a tough and smart businessman but, long story short, he eventually leant us the money at 10 percent interest. Once I knew we had the money, Kenny told me to low ball the offer to the S&L to see how they responded. Great lesson I learned because they responded with the number that I was prepared to buy the lots for, but Kenny told me that they would not give me their best price after only one counter. Needless to say, we ended up buying those 12 lots at $30,000 each, which was 33 percent of the loan amount. I left my father's business and Kenny and I started Tate Development Corporation 'TDC' in 1986." He concludes his story on his introduction to entrepreneurship by noting that "over the next three years, TDC successfully developed a multifamily residential project in Delray Beach; bought and developed a 40 acre thirty-five (35) luxury single family home community in Davie with the average home price being over $500,000 each; developed and leased (and still own today) 100,000 sq. ft. commercial shopping center in Weston; built luxury single family homes in Boca Raton; bought a 33,000 sq. ft. warehouse and converted it into a refrigerated warehouse and leased the entire building to a large produce distributer; and, of course, completed the 12 lots and built luxury homes averaging over $450,000 each in Jacaranda Cove, which is what started all of this. Tate Development Corporation has since developed, owned and operated over $500,000,000 in real estate since inception."

He begins his advice to aspiring entrepreneur with a quote from Sam Walton, "Capital is not scarce; vision is" and continues to say "hence, *vision* along with *creativity, versatility, passion, hunger, confidence* and a *positive attitude* are the characteristics that all successful entrepreneurs have in common." He also likes to quote Vince Lombardi as he puts it when explaining the importance of *hunger*, as follows; 'The difference between a successful person and others is not a lack of strength, not a lack of knowledge, but rather a lack of will." He continues "I would also share with any aspiring entrepreneur that, in order to be successful, you must be clear with your vision. Set your goals both short term and long term. Determine the best path for you, as an individual, to accomplish these goals as all paths are not the same. There are many ways to get to the top of the mountain." He cautions that "what worked for me may not work for someone else." And, he advises to "create an easily understood mission statement so your support staff clearly understands your mission, your objectives and your approach." He calls it the "Paint by Numbers" approach. He continues to say "keep it simple. Put together a good team (strong and loyal support staff) and get their buy in by offering them a piece of the action or good incentives so they feel like they are part of your vision. It is particularly important to have a quality, competent, hardworking, and diligent team that you can trust and count on." He concludes his advice to aspiring entrepreneurs by adding "lastly, you must create a realistic budget and cash flow analysis so you know how much working capital is needed to sustain your business (vision) plan until you can break even. Plan for the unexpected and add on additional working capital for same."

With respect to the areas of opportunities and innovation in construction and development, Jimmy states that "from time to time, each industry has its own imbalances and/or inefficiencies which rear their ugly head. It is in those same veins where opportunities exist and must be monetized through entrepreneurial innovation and creativity. It is therefore incumbent upon all business owners who possess the entrepreneurial spirit to foresee these imbalances and inefficiencies when they occur, identify the opportunities, and then professionally and proficiently act upon them." He goes on to add, as an example, that "in 2005-2006 when the single family home real estate markets around the country were growing exponentially, we felt that the growth was due to easy money directly related to poor lending practices. The banks had figured out a way to offer fast and easy single-family home mortgages for individual homeowners. Then the banks would warehouse these mortgages until such time as a Wall Street firm would take them and bundle them with other similar mortgage portfolios, thereby mitigating the risk of the larger portfolio. The Wall Street firms would then obtain a credit rating from a nationally recognized credit rating firm, such as Moody's, Fitch Ratings, and others, in an effort to increase the value of the Mortgage-Backed Securities. Then, Wall Street would sell these tranches of Mortgage-Backed Securities to the retail markets. These transactions were called Securitizations. The buyers were usually large financial institutions looking to get a good yield on their cash. Since each transaction generated big fees, everyone was making money and the best part for all the parties involved was that no one held the risk on their respective balance sheets for more than a month or two." What Jimmy is describing has since come to be known as the "Great Recession" caused by the country's housing crisis of the late 2000s. This is where Jimmy's entrepreneurial instincts kicked in as he continues to say "the problem as we saw it was that the mortgage brokers (originators of these loans) were not paying attention to the most important aspect of any single-family home mortgage and that was the qualification of the borrowers and the quality/value of the assets. The mortgage brokers only cared about earning their fees. The banks that actually made the initial mortgages did not care because, as mentioned earlier, they sold off their risk within a month or two and they also made their fees. Unfortunately, there were no policies and procedures in place to justify most, if not all, of these single-family home loan approvals and subsequent closings. No one cared because they all made their fees, and everyone was getting rich." He concludes his example by adding "we saw this as a major imbalance within the real estate market and, therefore, we saw it as an opportunity." Jimmy and his brother, Kenny, studied this segment of the market, determined where the opportunity could be, and then moved in that direction. Jimmy then reached out to his close friend, Sergio Rok, discussed the opportunities they saw, and convinced him to join the team as a partner. Sure enough, what followed was the housing market collapse and by studying the market and understanding the forces at work and having the foresight to act, Jimmy, his brother, Kenny, as well as partners, Sergio Rok and Jorge Perez, were able to take advantage and make money when most people were losing money. Another interesting anecdote that Jimmy shared is how he and Jorge Perez teamed up during this time. He goes on to recount "another savvy real estate developer by the name of Jorge Perez also saw similar opportunities and he called me to set up a meeting. We discussed our approaches to this unique commercial market opportunity. I quickly realized that, with his infrastructure, available cash, and expertise, he could only make the Tate/Rok team stronger; so, we welcomed Jorge and his Related Group on board. The rest is history, we (Tate, Rok and Perez) successfully acquired approximately 25 different distressed debt opportunities. All but one of these acquisitions turned into fee ownership. The total value of the assets we acquired ended up being worth well over a billion dollars. Ninety percent (90 percent) of our acquisitions were institutional grade commercial assets all around the country. The average acquisition price was approximately 30 cents on the dollar. Once we owned the debt, we would successfully negotiate with the borrowers to release them from their personal guarantees on the debt. In return, they would assign their membership interests in their borrowing entities to us and then, at the right time, we would affect a friendly deed in lieu of foreclosure whereby we would take control and direct ownership of the underlying asset. We then did what we do best. We asset managed, created value and, when the market heated up, we monetized our investments by selling into a strong growing market. As luck would have it, the one distressed mortgage for which we paid $100 million but had not yet taken control of the fee was the Omni property in downtown

Miami. Genting, a large multi-national billion-dollar gambling conglomerate, actually bought the B note and exercised their right to pay us off in full. The original note that we controlled was valued at approximately $162 million +/-, inclusive of accrued fees and penalties. A little luck never hurts!"

Jimmy believes that the best way to become an expert is "through trial and error." He adds that "the more experience you have, the smarter you become." He continues to advise "do not ever believe in get rich quick schemes. I am a research and data driven critical thinker. I listen to others and try to learn from their experiences because, at a young age, I realized that you are only as smart as your past experiences and, for most young professionals, you physically cannot have that many experiences simply as a function of age and time. Hence, the next best thing than your own experiences are the experiences of others in your field." He concludes by saying "learn from people's successes and, equally important, learn from other people's failures. The least expensive failure you can have is someone else's. As my father, Stanley Tate, used to tell me, 'Jimmy, don't let people know what you don't know. G-d has blessed you with two ears and one mouth. Keep things in that proportion.' In other words, keep your mouth shut and your ears open. The best lessons in life are free."

8. Media Relations

Entrepreneur: George Haj
Company: Haj Media
Specialty: Media relations

> *Be tenacious. Constantly network, constantly read and learn about your craft. Whether you have one client or 20, give each one the attention they deserve—and if you can't, don't take the business.*
>
> —George Haj

George is a media relations specialist who spent more than 30 years as a newspaper editor. After leaving his latest employer in 2017, he thought long and hard about returning to the troubled field of newspapers, and instead, after much consideration and thought, he decided that he would take the knowledge and experience gained throughout his career and channel it into creating a boutique media relations firm. He took the leap into entrepreneurship. Like many in the same position, he was unsure of how his journey would go, but he took the leap nonetheless and has not looked back.

George was born in New Jersey and moved to Miami when he was five years old. He and his wife, Jenna, split their time between Miami and Houston. His son, Alex, lives north of Dallas. He earned his bachelor's degree in communications from the University of Miami, and in 1999 to 2000, he was awarded a Knight Fellowship at Stanford University, where he studied international relations and business. He is the founder and president of Haj Media, a boutique media and marketing firm specializing in media strategy, crisis communications, and messaging for law firms, corporate clients, and nonprofits. He has written and spoken extensively on crisis communications and how companies of all sizes can navigate a fast-moving media environment. Before starting his own firm, he worked as a senior editor at the Miami Herald, Houston Chronicle, and ALM Media, parent company of legal publications such as American Lawyer. He was part of a Miami Herald team that won a Pulitzer Prize, directed work in Houston recognized as a Pulitzer finalist, and served on boards of numerous journalism organizations in Houston and around the nation.

George never really had the goal of becoming an entrepreneur. He explains it as "I'd love to say there was a grand plan but after leaving my last corporate position after 33 years in various newsrooms, I decided I didn't want to rejoin a troubled news business," so instead he decided to start his own firm. He goes on to say "I visited with everyone who would talk with me—friends, PR professionals, law firm leaders, CEOs, community leaders, and talked to them about their communications needs. Out of that came one client, then another, then a third and the work started growing." His story is like many, in that if you are good at what you do, people (clients) will find you no matter where you are. He continues his start-up story by saying "after one year, my one-person shop became two and we just hired a third and brought on an intern." He concludes by adding "There were no quick wins; work begat more work." Today, starting his fourth year, he has doubled revenue every year.

The advice he would give an aspiring entrepreneur in his field is that "nothing beats excellent writing skills. Learn to write compelling copy, whether it's for a web site, press release or internal communications. And invest the time to understand your client's needs." He adds that "You might have the best ideas in the world but if they are not aligned with the client's needs and desires, you won't be successful." He concludes by saying "above all, be tenacious. Constantly network, constantly read and learn about your craft. Whether you have one client or 20, give each one the attention they deserve—and if you can't, don't take the business."

George believes the areas of opportunities and innovation in media relations in working with law firms, corporate clients, and nonprofits lie in helping them effectively tell their stories. He explains that "much of that is still by 'pitching' stories to newspapers and TV stations for publication but now there are multiple avenues for firms to produce their own content and distribute them on a variety of channels, from their websites to Twitter, LinkedIn, Facebook and their own e-mail newsletters." He continues to add that "as mainstream media outlets continue to contract, helping firms tell their own story through their own channels is going to be critical."

George believes that the best way to become an expert in his field is to listen. He advises to "listen to other professionals who have come before you. Listen to your interns and young people in your organization about how they are communicating and how they are absorbing news and information. Listen to your clients to understand their *business* needs, not just their communications needs." He concludes by saying that you should "be willing to endlessly experiment."

9. Real Estate

Entrepreneur: Mario Avalos
Company: Kirilauscas & Associates
Specialty: Real estate agent

Invest money in your mind and surround yourself with people that are better than you in this trade.

—Mario Avalos

Mario is a real estate agent who has demonstrated resilience, perseverance, and determination. He embodies what it means to keep moving forward despite how many obstacles are placed in your way. He understands and displays unparalleled customer service and attention to detail and knows how to build trust with his clients.

Mario was born in Peru but was raised in Miami since the age of seven. He has been with his wife, Rosangela Kirilauscas, for 20 plus years and has three boys, Jake, Daniel, and Mateo, ages eight, five, and three, respectively. He attended Coral Gables high and graduated with, admittedly, a not so stellar GPA, putting him in a hole from the start. That was his first hurdle. He overcame that one and went on to graduate from Florida International University in 2001 with a Bachelor of Arts in finance. He began his career as a business analyst for Cordis (Johnson and Johnson). Five years later, in 2006, he realized that he had chosen the wrong career path, so he resigned and started his career over from scratch. That became his second hurdle. He then decided to become a real estate investor and try his hand at flipping homes. Sadly, during what history now refers to as the Great Recession, that included a housing and market collapse, he lost everything and once again had to start his career over from scratch. That became is third hurdle. In 2009, he decided to become a real estate agent, and since then. he has had a successful career and has never looked back. The last 12 months have been one of his most successful of his career having represented 124 transactions, many with notable clients. Mario owns and manages 15 rental units. He purchased four residential lots in 2019, of which he built-out and sold one of the lots and planned to break ground on the other three later in 2020. His brokerage firm, of which his wife is the broker, is among the top real estate listing offices for foreclosed assets in Southeast Florida. They represent Coastland Construction, located in Pinecrest, in the sale of their new construction projects, including their upcoming Vista Lago complex consisting of 113 townhouses and 230 condos in Miami Gardens. Mario has been involved in the community as prior Rotarian for the Rotary Club of Dadeland and the Rotary Club of South Miami. He has supported numerous scholarships and volunteered for events benefiting low-income youth, including Host A Hero, an organization that fully funds veterans' vacations, including their immediate family members.

Mario never really had the goal of becoming an entrepreneur. Entrepreneurship, in Mario's case is exemplified by his mental toughness. He goes on to say: "I had a great upbringing with awesome parents. Had a fun life thru high school and college. I was a great employee at Cordis. I made great money flipping homes. And I had all the confidence in the world." Then, reality hit him when the market crashed. Now he realizes that more so than the financial loss that he suffered, it was the mental injury that he was not prepared to deal with. He credits his wife, his self-awareness, and his faith for providing him with the strength to overcome the mental obstacles, as he puts it "in order to start making decisions to better our lives."

The advice he would give an aspiring entrepreneur in his field is "to find 2 or 3 realtors to follow their everyday activities for several months. Observe what they do to generate money day in day out. And then determine if what you see motivates you to get into the business." He adds that "according to the National Association of Realtors, failure rate in our industry is 87 percent within the first two years on being in business across the country." He believes that the reason for this is a huge misunderstanding of the work needed to become successful. He admits that he wanted to quit the business every day during his first year. He acknowledges that he had a "foggy illusion of easy work, easy money." After all, during the height of the market, it seemed to him that half the people he knew, and their family members, all had licenses. He continues to add that "the media, at the time, portrayed a great lifestyle and made it look so easy."

Mario believes the areas of opportunities and innovation in real estate are "that of consolidating a very fragmented process." He goes on to add that "when someone buys or sells a property, not only are there too many vendors or entities involved in the process, but they are also moving at different speeds and directions." This, he says, "can create a lot of unnecessary and unpredictability in the outcome." He concludes by saying, after providing a few examples, that "the opportunity of innovation lays on somehow consolidating where and how data is extracted at a cost low enough that no longer prevents vendors from performing their tasks without regard to sequence."

Mario believes that the best way to become an expert in his field is to "invest money in your mind and surround yourself [with] people that are better than you in this trade." He goes on to provide an example of how he was able to land a developer as a client by hiring consultants to help secure the project as well as to help him navigate problems as they came up. He understood his limitations and sought help. He also highly recommends focusing on converting leads, as opposed to generating leads. He admits that "at first, we were generating lots of leads with low 'conversion' rate. Now we generate less leads with higher conversion rate" As he explains, he was able to accomplish this by "learning what to say, how to say and when to say it when talking to prospects. In other words, we invested in our minds."

10. Photography

Entrepreneur: Walter Aleman
Company: Walter Aleman Photography and Events
Specialty: Event photography

Learning the business aspect of photography was the key factor in my success...there is so much more to learn then just clicking the shutter.
                                                —Walter Aleman

Walter is a specialty photographer. He focuses on wedding and event photography and videography. He started in photography using the traditional art of the dark room when it took a considerable investment of time simply to see how one image would turn out. He is the epitome of hard work and determination. He understands the meaning of paying your dues and earning your way, regardless of what it takes. He has demonstrated that he is willing to sacrifice to get to the next level.

Walter was born in Yonkers, New York, but was raised in the Jackson Heights neighborhood in Queens. He then moved to Miami to attend high school and college. He studied studio art and photography and earned his Bachelor of Arts from Florida Atlantic University. He also attended the Art Institute of Ft. Lauderdale to learn the business aspect of photography. He started his own photography business in 2015 after many years of paying his dues, oftentimes assisting other photographers, and shooting events for free to gain the experience and recognition necessary to go out on his own. In March of 2020, Walter's firm received the 2020 WeddingWire Couples' Choice Awards, an accolade representing the top wedding professionals across the board in quality, service, responsiveness, and professionalism reviewed by couples on Wedding-Wire, an honor that has been bestowed on his firm for three years in a row. His firm also was bestowed the 2020 "Knot Best of Weddings" award at the Fourteenth Annual Best of Weddings Awards, honoring the top wedding vendors across America for the second year in a row. In 2020, only 5 percent of hundreds of thousands of local wedding professionals listed on the Knot received this distinguished award. Walter and his firm have also been very active in the community, having supported, volunteered and/or provided pro bono services for such causes as the Make a Wish Foundation, Best Buddies, Selfless Love Foundation, Cuban American Bar Association, Broward Public Library Foundation, The City Of North Lauderdale Recreation Foundation, to name a few.

Walter decided to become an entrepreneur after much hard work and sacrifice. As he recalls, "I reached out to the best 3 companies in South Florida that work on weddings. I told them I would work for free and was willing to learn." Walter interned without pay for a full year before he charged for his services. He saved enough money, with jobs he had on the side, to buy his own gear. Once he had his own gear, he offered to work as a second photographer for those same companies. He did that for five years while he built up his experience and clientele base. He managed to develop a good following among his friends who promoted his services through word of mouth. He goes on to say that "my personality is what really sells; however, my work showed my passion for creating moments." That is when he decided to take the leap into entrepreneurship. To this day, he collaborates, from time to time, with the same three companies with whom he got his start.

The advice he would give an aspiring entrepreneur in the photography industry is to "dream big, have a vision of what you want to do in photography." He emphasizes the importance of taking a course on the business aspect of photography. He states, "Learning the business aspect of photography was the key factor in my success." He goes on to say that "there is so much more to learn then just clicking the shutter." He also highly recommends getting an internship. He says that you should "learn from others who have the experience…learning is always the key." He concludes by saying that "everyone has their own style. You have to find yours. One must learn the ability to adapt and be resourceful in unexpected situations…look at the view finder with a creative eye… think imaginatively but also strategically."

Walter believes the areas of opportunities and innovation in photography lie in having the "confidence to take on big, ambitious goals and take risks when shooting…being different than the other photographers." He also believes it is innovative to share and collaborate with other photographers, instead of obsessively guarding your secrets and techniques. He believes his photography is an art form meant to be shared with anyone who wants to learn the craft.

Walter believes that the best way to become an expert in photography, regardless of the type or subject matter, is to "find your niche, then become amazing at it." He continues that you should "do your homework. Look at what's trending, see what other photographers are saying. Go to meetings, join photography organizations." He reemphasizes the importance of finding a mentor and states that his mentor is still his best friend to this day and concludes that his mentor "is the reason I am the photographer I am."

11. Politics

Entrepreneur: Juan Carlos (J.C.) Bermudez
Company: City of Doral
Specialty: Mayor

> *One should be a public servant if he or she believes they can bring about positive change for their community, keep an open ear to all and make the best decision possible for your community based on facts.*
> —Juan Carlos (J.C.) Bermudez

J.C. is the Mayor of the city of Doral located in South Florida. He is a man of his word. He got involved in politics not for fame, power, or wealth, but to help his family and his community. He has demonstrated his commitment to both in his time at office. It is rare these days to find a politician that not only keeps his word but truly cares deeply about his community and lets his actions do most of the talking. Not only did he effectively lead his city through its conception and incorporation in 2003, by acquiring and building new parks, schools and infrastructure, but he is currently knee-deep in the mist of passionately and tirelessly leading his city through the current medical and financial crisis caused by the epic global pandemic (COVID-19). In both instances, he has managed to give selflessly of himself to assist and improve his city and the lives of its residents along the way. For this reason, and many more, the city of Doral has recently decided to bestow the great honor of naming one of its high schools after him, The J.C. Bermudez Doral Senior High School.

J.C. was born in Santa Clara, Cuba. His family moved from Cuba to the United States in December of 1965 on one of the first "Freedom Flights" under the Lyndon B. Johnson administration. Previously, his older brother had moved to the United States, alone, in 1962, soon after J.C. was born, through the Peter Pan Program, a clandestine program of the Archdiocese of Miami where children came to the United States with the help of the Catholic Church. He and his family left Cuba, like many others, because the Cuban Dictatorship had confiscated the personal property of its citizens and denied them the basic human rights required in an open society. J.C. grew up in Hialeah, Fl. He is married to his wife, Vivian, a special education teacher, and together they have three daughters (Eneida Marie, Elena Catherine, and Elisa Nicole). J.C. earned a Bachelor of Arts degree from the University of Miami and a law degree (Juris doctorate) from the University of Notre Dame Law School. He has practiced law in South Florida for over 30 years. In 2003, J.C. was elected the first ever Mayor of the then newly incorporated city of Doral, in South Florida. He served as mayor of the city for the first 9.5 years of its existence, through 2012. In 2016, he was re-elected by the residents of Doral and returned to office where he currently serves, once again, as the Mayor. J.C. is a past president (2010–2011) of the Miami-Dade County League of Cities, and throughout his tenure as a mayor, he has served as a Board Member of the Florida League of Cities, Florida League of Mayors, and the U.S. Conference of Mayors where he also chaired the International Affairs committee. Additionally, J.C. served on the Beacon Council Board and received the Good Government Award from the Greater

Miami Chamber of commerce in 2009. He is currently a member of the U.S. Conference of Mayors Advisory Board, the Florida league of Mayors Board, as well as the Miami-Dade County Transportation Planning Organization Board. Under his leadership, the city of Doral added over 121 acres of playgrounds, ball fields, and recreational facilities while purchasing, through grants and funds, an additional 45 acres of parkland, all the while creating the new city's infrastructure. During J.C.'s terms, the city has received numerous national accolades, including being chosen the Best City for Business Start Ups (*Business Week*), named #2 of America's top 25 Towns to live well in for its cultural amenities, pro-business environment, and highly educated workforce (Forbes.com), named the third best place in the United States to retire (*US News* and *World Report*) and was ranked the 51st best in top 100 places to live and launch a business in the United States (CNNMoney.com). Most recently, the City of Doral was named the fastest growing city in Florida and 11th in the country by the Florida International University's Metropolitan Center. Working with the Miami-Dade County School Board and local PTAs and PTOs, Doral was the only city in Miami-Dade County to have all of its public schools rated "A Schools" during J.C.'s tenure as the Mayor. J.C. currently works at SMGQ Law in Coral Gables, Florida, and practices in the area of business and corporate transactions, real estate, government and public policy law. Aside from all of his community involvement, as mayor of the city of Doral, J.C. is also personally involved in his community. He is a member of the University of Miami Citizens Board, The Doral Contemporary Art Museum (DORCAM), and is a founding member and part of the Parish Council at Our Lady of Guadalupe Catholic Church in Doral.

J.C. Believes that the areas and opportunities of innovation in politics lie in the areas of technology. He starts by saying "I think that public service is one of the most rewarding things that you can do." He continues by adding "Having said that, technology has changed everything, from campaigning to how you serve your community and constituents." He says that "The newer platforms are now needed to reach voters and residents." Because, he adds, "Technology allows an elected official to keep his or her community informed in real time about decisions that affect them. This includes legislation, events and even emergencies such as impending hurricanes or the COVID-19 crisis." He believes that "…Mayors, who are on the front lines, and the elected officials closest to the community, will need to really be able to use the different social media platforms to get their message out." He cautions, however, that "At the same time, this can be a double-edged sword as people can publish anything they want without verification and the elected leader must and should be able to refute those untruths in all platforms." J.C. also believes that the areas of greatest need, which can make the most immediate impact, if someone wants to get involved in politics, is to get involved at the local level. He believes that is the easiest way to impact people's lives directly. He recommends to "…start on a city, town, village or even community board." By either appointment or running for office. He cautions, however, that "The key is to get involved for the right reasons. If you believe you can make a change or help, then you should do it." He adds, "Don't do it to improve your business or to see your name on a ballot. Those are the wrong reasons." J.C. believes that "…the reason for the involvement is as important as the involvement itself. If you truly believe that you can make a difference do it. Keep in mind that if you do it the right way it is very fulfilling." He concludes his advice on getting involved in politics by saying "Very rarely can you impact things as dramatically as being a policy maker at whatever level you choose. I think that too many people today are dissuaded from being part of this process because of the bad reputation politics has gotten today. If done the right way, for the right reasons it can be one of the most rewarding experiences in life."

J.C. believes that the best advice he can give an aspiring politician is "One should be a public servant if he or she believes they can bring about positive change for their community, keep an open ear to all and make the best decision possible for your community based on facts." He warns, however, and adds that "One other thing is—have a thick skin. Being elected in today's climate of unfounded information means that your life, and your families, will become an open book and your opponents, in general, will certainly use what they can against you, even anonymously on these new social media portals, when they can." He concludes by saying "This is difficult for anyone and more so for your children, spouse and loved ones." With respect to his advice on how to get started as a politician he says, "There really is no better way than being in the fray." He continues "You can study political science, as I did, but the reality is that either working for an elected official or in government is the only other preparation." He admits his was an unusual circumstance, and that "I took no course on being a person who as a mayor founded a city from scratch. I just had to work hard, analyze lots of material and make the best decisions possible." With respect to entrepreneurs getting involved in politics, as a profession, J.C. states "I think that entrepreneurs should get involved in politics because real world experience is a great asset to have as a policy maker. Too many people go into politics without understanding that a government, like a business or a family, has to live within its means." He continues by saying "Businesspeople, and entrepreneurs in particular, know what it is to be creative, to think out of the box, to be efficient and effective with money while focusing on productive and realistic goals." He adds, "Thus, the business or entrepreneurship experience is an asset to any policy maker." He concludes by saying that "My time running my own law practice before I was an elected official helped prepare me for handling budgets, a staff, making decisions, running meetings and advocating for my community amongst many other things."

J.C.'s recollection and response to what has been his most fulfilling or rewarding experiences as a politician is to say "...there have been many, and some difficult moments, but the one that stands out the most is building a community, which we call a city, from scratch." He adds that "There are many Mayors across America but very few who get to be the founding mayor and see a 'place' become a community." He continues by saying that "When a young man, or woman, comes back to Doral after having gone away to school and reminds me of something I said in the middle school or high school graduation and how it impacted them and how proud they are of this city called Doral I feel great..." He concludes "...because it was not just a city we helped build but a community with a name and a culture that people can be proud of."

J.C. never really intended to run for public office, nor did he ever aspire to get involved in politics. He admits that the real reason he got involved, politically, and ran for office is "...because there were no parks for my children, badly maintained roads, not enough schools etc." He further states "I had never run for office or worked for government so I just did what anyone in democracy would do—I knocked on doors, met with neighbors and told them why I was running for Mayor!" As you can see from J.C.'s bio and accomplishments, while mayor of the city of Doral, he is a man of his word. He, along with his administration, created safe parks, good schools, and improved the city's infrastructure. Because of that one decision, by one individual, the city of Doral has made incredible strides and has made a positive impact on so many people's lives. Stories such as these are what should inspire individuals to get involved in politics, especially in the politically charged times we live in today.

12. Philanthropy

Entrepreneur: Ana VeigaMilton
Company: José Milton Foundation and United Property Management
Specialty: Giving back to the community

> *Being involved in one's community makes good business sense and is a positive way to activate one's brand on a broad scale while enjoying the feeling of contributing and helping others.*
>
> —Ana VeigaMilton

Ana has degrees in engineering and law and could achieve any goal and any measure of success in the corporate world if she so desired. However, instead of pursuing those careers to enrich herself further, she has instead decided to channel her efforts into giving back to the community and helping to enrich the lives of others. She has chosen to do this as a philanthropist, through her family's charitable foundation, the José Milton Foundation. She is extremely smart, outgoing, and has a great heart. She embodies what it means to give back.

Ana was born in Cuba and emigrated to the United States with her parents as a baby. She is married to her husband, Cecil, and has three children, all young adults, Alec, Diana, and Eric. She is a proud graduate of the Miami-Dade County Public School system, attending Southwest Miami High, where she graduated as valedictorian. She earned both an engineering and a law degree from the University of Miami, attending under academic merit scholarships. After earning her engineering degree, she worked for BellSouth as a telecommunications engineer while pursuing her Master of Science in Electrical Engineering from Florida

International University. After graduating from law school and passing the Florida Bar exam, she worked pro bono before becoming a full-time mom of three and dedicating herself to community service and philanthropy. She now serves as the president of the José Milton Foundation and as Corporate Social Responsibility Officer of United Property Management, the family real estate business. The José Milton Foundation was established by Ana's father-in-law to support programs and organizations in South Florida that improve the quality of life and close the opportunity gap, with a special focus on education, research, and health care. The Milton family business, United Property Management, is one of the largest property owners and managers in South Florida, with almost 8,000 residential units and commercial real estate. She guides the philanthropic, volunteer, and engagement efforts for her family and her business associates. Her accomplishments and accolades in these endeavors are too many to mention, and her involvement in the community is unparalleled. Some of her more notable accomplishments include being honored by Big Brothers Big Sisters as a Miracle Maker in 2011, by Chapman Partnership in 2012, and by the American Cancer Society's Inner Circle of Twelve in 2013. Ana received the Florida Blue Philanthropy Award at the American Red Cross Spectrum Luncheon and was a Plaza Health Network Foundation's Women of Distinction & Caring honoree. She was also honored by Miami Women Who Rock in 2017, as well as with the Education Fund's prestigious Sapoznik Insurance Public School Alumni Achievement Award in 2018. Most recently, Ana received the Mayor's Community Spirit Award from the Parks Foundation's *In the Company of Women* Awards. She was also proud to be inducted into the M-DCPS Alumni Hall of Fame and the UM College of Engineering presented Ana with the Dean's Innovation Award. A sample of her community involvement consists of Emeritus Board member of Zoo Miami Foundation, Executive Board member of the United Way, Executive Board member of the Jackson Health Foundation, member of the Miracle Society of Big Brothers Big Sisters, member of the American Red Cross Tiffany Circle and Board, and most notably, she is a member of the University of Miami Board of Trustees.

Ana believes that for someone wanting to give back and make an impact, the areas of greatest need are those that come "with the goal of improving the future." She emphasizes and states that one should focus on "those related to closing or eliminating the opportunity gap." She says that "through philanthropy, engagement, and mentoring, children of low socioeconomic standing and their families may access the tools that encourage learning & experimentation, promote a solid work ethic, and impart soft skills & socialization." She adds that "mentoring can help instill a love of learning which is so important for growth beyond the adolescent and young adult years. Curiosity needs to be encouraged, but for learning to happen, basic needs must be met, which means addressing the family and the community—access to healthcare, healthy practices, stability at home." She goes on to add that "for more immediate impact, scholarships for college students will allow academically talented students to pursue learning and experiences that lead to lucrative jobs and self-sufficiency." She stresses that "I particularly like to encourage minority students to study STEM, especially tech fields like engineering, for opportunities at high-paying internships and careers." She mentions that "scholarships for students entering accredited trade schools and certificate programs are also impactful as not every student can or should invest in a more formal college education. Qualified tradespeople are in high demand and help move society forward."

Ana believes that entrepreneurs should get involved in giving back to the community and their profession because "being involved in one's community makes good business sense and is a positive way to activate one's brand on a broad scale while enjoying the feeling of contributing and helping others." She states that by getting involved in community and with charitable organizations as well as your local university or college, public or private schools, and other nonprofit groups aiming at helping the community, "entrepreneurs can connect with new people—other business people, philanthropists, high net worth individuals, government officials—and get to know the needs of the community." She stresses that "Millennials and Gen Z individuals, both consumers/clients and employees, demand social impact and look to connect with viable businesses that care about people, community, and the environment – the triple bottom line of people, planet, and profits. Therefore, having a brand associated with social impact, addressing local as well as global issues, may help attract and retain talent and clients/customers. Doing well by doing good!" She concludes that "connecting to the community in a way consistent with your business model and integrating social impact into the company's values infuses the brand with meaning and depth."

One of the most fulfilling and rewarding experiences as a philanthropist, for Ana, has been involving her family in mentoring students who have been awarded the José Milton Foundation Advancing Minorities in STEM Scholarships. She says this "is very fulfilling as you see the positive, life-changing impact my family can have on a young person's future. The Milton STEM Scholarships are awarded to underserved, talented students who graduate from the 5000 Role Models of Excellence Program within Miami-Dade County Public Schools. These students are on their way to a successful academic experience, but with the added support provided by the Milton STEM Scholarship, the students can focus on learning." She is especially proud and recalls a moment when one STEM scholar texted her the following message: "Thank you so much for encouragement! It means a lot to know that people are excited for my success." She concludes that "when scholarship dollars are combined with mentoring, the investment pays off dividends and the experience is extremely gratifying."

Ana has always enjoyed being involved in her school and community, and as she puts it, "am driven to share my gratitude for the life and family I am so fortunate to have." She states, "I am pragmatic and understand that we are all connected and need to collaborate, find strength in diversity, and cooperate to make our community better, encouraging every member to rise to his/her potential." Ana started giving back in high school, raising money for school activities, and volunteering with community agencies. Once she had kids, she volunteered at their schools so as "to meet the parents and faculty and stay close to my own kids and their friends, all to create a community of support and friendship and improve the educational experience." Her first experience with formal philanthropy started at the Zoo Miami Foundation, where she volunteered for a committee and eventually joined and chaired the board. She states that "board service is gratifying, builds leadership skills, affords professional development, and connected me to the community and an important economic driver and family/community builder as well as STEM-educator in my county. By leveraging my resources, both personal and through the family business, and connecting our associates and friends to Zoo

Miami, I have exalted my brand as a force for conservation and education and have provided funds and friends to Zoo Miami while having a lot of fun along my journey." She concludes that "as my brand and my friends grew, I was asked to participate in other programs and orgs that build community and help close the opportunity gap, and now I select where and when to invest time, talent, treasure, and my sphere of influence and connections to address societal problems I feel I can best impact."

13. The Significant Other

Significant Other: Frances G. De La Guardia
Entrepreneurial Association: Wife of author or entrepreneur
Specialty: Supporter and advisor to an entrepreneur

> *Together with open eyes and open dialogue, the business and the partnership will succeed simultaneously.*
>
> *To assist in making someone's dream is the best part of the entire process because you get to see your loved one's dream realized and are part of that accomplishment.*
>
> —Frances G. De La Guardia

Frances is the author's or entrepreneur's wife, and this piece may actually be the most important of all, as it comes from the perspective of the individual that more than likely, you have pledged your life to, for better or for worse. The importance of this often overlooked perspective cannot be overstated, and it hits home because it was not until I asked her to write this piece that I fully understood what she went through and how I could have done better. I hope that every aspiring entrepreneur reads this piece carefully and does a better job than I did in making their significant other feel a part of the dream and more fully engaged and informed. It is never too late to learn and grow from your mistakes.

Frances was born in Miami Beach, Florida, at St. Francis Hospital but raised in Hialeah, Florida. Her mother and father, Betty Diaz and Jose A. Fernandez, were Cuban immigrants who fled to Miami in 1961 from Communist Cuba. They were a young recently married couple, both only children, who had immigrated to the United States under the sponsorship of her father's American-born aunt who lived in Key West, Florida. Both parents left their parents in Cuba when they fled to the United States. Frances has two sons, William and Nicholas. She attended Deerborne High School, a private school, in Coral Gables, Florida. She earned a Bachelor of Arts in Sociology from the University of Miami and followed that with a law degree from St. Thomas University School of Law. Her first job as an attorney was for a pilot program where attorneys worked as law clerks for circuit court judges in the 17th Judicial Circuit Court of Broward County, Florida. Frances clerked for five circuit court judges during the two-year clerkship program. In 1990, she began her advocacy career as a litigation attorney at a mid-sized insurance defense firm in Miami. While practicing at that insurance defense firm, Frances developed and honed her litigation skills and conducted jury trials along-side the senior managing partner. During her three years at that litigation firm, she began her appellate advocacy practice and fell in love with the practice of appellate law. The practice combined the academic aspects of research and writing with an advocacy component. After the birth of her first son, William, she began a judicial clerkship as staff attorney for the Honorable Judge Melvia Green at the Third District Court of Appeal in Miami. During her time at the court she had her second child Nicholas. Following her clerkship, Frances was recruited and hired to work as in-house counsel for State Farm Insurance Company Clams Litigation Counsel offices in Miami. She helped head the appellate section of the law firm and eventually became the head of the appellate department for the South Florida legal offices for State Farm Insurance Company. She spent seven years working as in-house counsel for State Farm Insurance until 2006 when she was recruited and hired to work for the international law firm of Holland & Knight, LLP (H&K) by Rodolfo Sorondo Jr., a former appellate judge of the Third District Court of Appeal. She joined the firm as senior counsel in the appellate litigation group. After two years as senior counsel, she was promoted to partner at the firm where she currently works to this day. During her last 13 years with H&K, she has received the following recognitions: from 2007 to 2009, she was recognized as a Florida Legal Elite Lawyer in appellate law by the *Florida Trend* magazine. In 2010 and 2015, she was selected as the Most Effective Lawyer finalist by the *Daily Business Review*. From 2016 to 2020, she has been selected as a Florida Super Lawyer by the *Florida Super Lawyers* magazine. In 2017, she was nationally recognized with her firm's "Living the Commitment Award" for her pro bono and charitable client services. In 2018, she was honored with the Amicus Service Award by the International Municipal Lawyers Association for her legal advocacy. In addition to her service to her clients and her firm, she also has an outstanding record of community service. Her pro bono work includes representing asylum applicants on behalf of Catholic Charities, working with Legal Services of Greater Miami's Hurricane Relief Clinics Charity in the Florida Keys to assist victims of Hurricane IRMA, and traveling to Puerto Rico to assist victims of Hurricane Maria with their insurance claims. In 2014, Frances was appointed Alumni Association President for the St. Thomas University School of Law and also serves on the Law School's Advisory Board. In 2015, she was elected to the board of directors of the Cuban American Bar Association (CABA) where throughout the years, she served on numerous committees, was chief editor of the CABA Briefs magazine, was elected as secretary, vice president, and then, in 2019, she was elected as the President-Elect of CABA. While serving as president-elect of CABA, in 2019, she served as president of one of CABA's two charitable arms, CABA Pro Bono, which advocates for unaccompanied minors, veterans, and victims of domestic violence and human trafficking. She began her leadership term as the President of CABA in 2020 when she was sworn in at one of the most successful installation galas in the history of the organization with over 1,100 persons in attendance and a record number of funds raised for CABA's two charitable arms (CABA Pro Bono and CABA Foundation). She began her term with tremendous success and then had to pivot and temporarily reinvent the organization to adapt to the challenges of the 2020 global pandemic COVID-19.

Frances' advice to both an aspiring entrepreneur and the significant other of an aspiring entrepreneur before they start their journey is, first, to the entrepreneur: "have a detailed business plan and discuss that plan with your spouse or partner." She adds that you should "Be candid and frank in that discussion and consider the reality that any dream of being an entrepreneur comes with sacrifices both monetary and emotional." She believes that "The planning of a new business is a challenging process and because it does not happen overnight, it requires an open line of communication with your spouse regarding goals and a realistic time-line to achieve those goals." She goes on to say that "The conversations and discussions have to be constant and open and must include the hard discussions of how you will financially manage the business, what you will you do if the first attempt fails or if you encounter obstacles." To the significant other, she advises that "Because there will be roadblocks and issues, as the partner of the entrepreneur, you must be open-minded and be part of the decision making process and have the knowledge neces-sary to face those obstacles when they arise." She continues saying that "together with open eyes and open dialogue, the business and the partner-ship will succeed simultaneously." Finally, she says that "My advice is for the partner to ask questions and set goals of communication beforehand and to keep that dialogue open from the inception and throughout the duration of the business."

Frances recalls that during the start-up process, of which she nudged her husband to embark on, she became aware of "The amount of time it takes to build a business and that once it is built you still have to keep working at it day after day." She adds "It's an ongoing process each year, depending on the economy or what is happening in the world." She con-tinues to say, "For instance, with the pandemic, this year, business owners have had to reinvent and adapt their goals and ideas to fit the challenging times." She adds, from experience, that "The partner of the entrepreneur has to be prepared to have financial lows and debt, short term and long term, during the inception and during the continuation of the business." She continues that "Because of these economic struggles, it is important to have long range plans and back up plans in case the business has to be temporarily downsized or reimagined. Thus, the partner of the entrepre-neur must have flexibility and understanding as well as being supportive of the idea and the dream." She further states that "It is a fine line to walk to be inspirational and yet provide honest practical opinions that may not be what the person with the dream wants to hear." She concludes by say-ing that "It can be done; however, it is best done when the conversation of these possibilities is discussed before the start of the business."

Frances believes that the most difficult aspect of being the significant other of an entrepreneur or ambitious individual is "Being an observer and not having an active part in the decision making process on a business you helped build, either because you gave monetary or emotional contributions to make the business possible." She adds that "Being the partner of the entrepreneur requires you to have many roles; that of a supporter, of a financial sounding board, a psychologist, and a friend and none of these roles are easy to undertake." She continues by saying that "My advice would be to be optimistic and keep your eye on the prize and that the outcome is the legacy and pride of being part of building not just a business, but a dream." She concludes by saying that "To assist in making someone's dream is the best part of the entire process because you get to see your loved one's dream realized and are part of that accomplishment."

Frances believes that one of the most fulfilling or rewarding experiences as the significant other of an entrepreneur or ambitious individual is to "see your partner enjoy the success from his hard work and when he receives the accolades he deserves for making a plan, seeing it through and then passing on that knowledge to new entrepreneurs." Another fulfillment is to witness her partner's "commitment to his dream and the desire to teach others what he learned, to help them achieve their dreams." She continues to add that "Perhaps the most surprising reward is to be witness to the evolution of the dream and see it become more than either of you imagined or planned." And, while she admits that "the evolution is not something you foresee or even plan for at the beginning, it is certainly one of the most fulfilling emotions you will ever feel." She concludes that "despite all the trials and tribulations and missteps that will occur, the end result of seeing a partner's dream and business come to fruition makes it all worth it."

Chapter 8: Specialize and Become an Expert

Recommended Activities

1. Make a list of all potential areas of specialty of interest to you. Speak to successful people in those areas and pick their brain on how to become an expert in that field.
2. Make a list of products or services, in that particular specialty, that you feel can be improved. Use the meditation techniques of Chapter 2 (What do Entrepreneurs Think About?), the sections on thinking for ideas and thinking to solve a problem.
3. Identify ways to set yourself apart from your competition by creating credentials. Make a list of credentials that you can earn to enhance your credibility.
4. Have a frank conversation with your significant other about their thoughts on you pursuing entrepreneurship and the associated risks.

CHAPTER 9

Do Not Be Afraid to Fail

Lack of success is proportionately related
to lack of effort and preparation.

This chapter will focus on the concept of failure and how to mitigate it. Failure is defined as: "the lack of success." The main obstacle to success is fear of failure. Failure, success, and fear work hand in hand. However, because, as mentioned in Chapter 4, everyone's definition of success is different, failure too will have a different meaning for different people and there are different ways to mitigate fear of failure. The second biggest deterrent to entrepreneurship, aside from the start-up funding aspect is avoidance of failure. As with fear and avoidance of risk, discussed in Chapter 5 (Do Not be Afraid to Take Risks), the first part of that combination, fear, is natural, and you can learn to channel it. The second part of that combination, avoidance, is counterproductive. It means you are not confronting or dealing with an issue. You are missing out on potential learning opportunities. Do not attempt to avoid failure because it will happen. Besides, it is a lot easier to avoid risk then it is to avoid failure. Many people, can, and do, go through life having avoided risk, but very few people can avoid failure. Those that prepare the most and mitigate it the best, will have a better chance at success. How you handle failure, or challenging times, is determined by the amount of experience or intuition that you have and is a byproduct of preparation. Some say you should hope for the best but plan for the worst. Once again, like in the space program, first mentioned in Chapter 5 (Do Not be Afraid to Take Risks), the fear of failure did not stop our scientist from reaching for and attaining the goal of landing on the moon. They failed many times, but learned from each failure and got better. They prepared, planned, tested, researched, and pushed forward, despite their previous failures.

Their fears forced them to plan for all contingencies and triple-check all their numbers. There was too much at risk, not to.

The first step in dealing with failure is to understand it. As the definition of failure is "the lack of success," and as the definition of success is different for everyone, you must first define what success means to you. The next step, based on your definition of success, is then to identify and define what failure means to you. There are two forms of failure: professional failure and personal failure. There is only one way to mitigate failure, that is, through preparation. There is only one way to benefit from failure, that is, by learning from it.

What is your definition of failure? As failure is lack of success, first you must define success by identifying your ultimate goal. The lack of obtaining your ultimate goal, by your own definition, is failure. This definition can be redefined and adjusted over time. Refer to Chapter 4 (Identify and Attain Your Goals). Failure then, will be the lack of "enter your definition of success here." Once you understand what failure is, you can plan for it and learn to mitigate it. However, failure is not relegated solely to lack of achieving your ultimate goal alone, along with your ultimate goal, you should have subgoals designed to attain your ultimate goals; therefore, failure, too, will be defined by the lack of attaining each of those subgoals. Therefore, you will have many opportunities at both success and failure in your path to your ultimate goal (success). The point is, to be successful, or attain lack of failure, you must be keenly aware of all of your subgoals and prepare and plan accordingly. This is done by, as mentioned in Chapter 4 (Identify and Attain Your Goals), identifying all your sub goals, writing them down, planning, creating action items and tracking your progress. They should be extremely specific, attainable action items and be set to manageable deadlines. Then, think of ways in which you can fail in attaining each of the subgoals. Once you have done that, include ways to mitigate failure of attaining each subgoal and be prepared.

What are you afraid of? If you have a fear of failure, following the preceding suggestion will help mitigate that. You must understand that fear of failure, as well as fear of anything, is a defense mechanism. Your body will physically and literally warn you of impending harm. That fear and those physical effects will force you, if you focus its energy properly, to prepare better than you normally would. It is your mind cautioning you that you are leaving your comfort zone and heading into the unknown. It is okay and natural to be afraid. You must pay attention to its cues and act accordingly. Learn to channel that fear into preparation and do not let it paralyze you. Once you understand what your fear of failure entails, then you should write down the rest of your fears and study them and then confront them in the same manner. Define them, understand them, break them down, and create a plan to mitigate them.

Professional failure: Lack of business success:

1. *Prepare*: The only way to mitigate failure or achieve success is to be prepared. You must thoroughly understand the subject matter. Like mentioned in Chapter 5 (Do Not be Afraid to Take Risks), learning to mitigate failure is like preparing for a test. If you listen in class, do the homework assignments, and read the assigned books, the odds are in your favor that you will not fail. The same is true of preparing for failures. You must also understand the consequences of you failing. You must have a mitigation plan ready. An exit strategy. Perform a risk of failure assessment. Do your research and homework and understand what you are getting yourself into. Make a list of all the potential consequences associated with failure. It is said that success happens when opportunity meets preparation. I would add…and a little luck. There is also no guarantee that good planning will lead to success. But, by planning for success, you mitigate failure.

2. *Learn*: The only way to benefit from failure is to learn from it and do not repeat the same mistakes that led you down that path to that result. If you do fail, you must learn from it and grow. Times of failure force you to take measure and stock of yourself. It exposes weakness that need improvement. Failure shows you what you are made of and how you react to adversity and, if and how, you overcome, will be a testament to your character. Sometimes, you learn more from your failures than you do from your successes. Times of success, while very gratifying, are easy to digest for you and your friends and family. Times of failure are not easy to digest, and they can expose tensions and vulnerabilities. They can, however, if analyzed and understood properly, offer up paths and opportunities to

improvement that are not readily available after times of success. So, in a weird way, failure is good, if it provides you with a valuable lesson. It can allow you to redefine failure and recategorize it as a learning experience. Why should you not avoid failure? Because you will deprive yourself of a valuable learning opportunity though real-life experience. Resilience and sacrifice are essential to recovering from and learning from failure. Not getting discouraged or giving up, but instead steeling of resolve and determination are key traits of successful entrepreneurs and accomplished people in general.

Personal failure: Lack of personal success or the effects of professional failure on your personal life.

1. *Be open with your family and loved ones*: The lack of business success can affect and lead to personal failures if you allow it. Exposure to failure can grow like a cancer if not dealt with properly. Those affects are not limited to the entrepreneur, but affect everyone. This can also create risk or exposure to mental injury. Talk openly about the upcoming risks and the consequences of failing and how you have planned for it. Discuss the sacrifices you will be expected to make. Being open about the hardships and struggles you can face, or are facing, is one way to lessen the emotional burden. Do not hide those feelings from you family or loved ones.

2. *Create an advisory group*: Entrepreneurs understand that they do not know everything, so they surround themselves with advisors in all fields of practice to consult and seek advice from. This includes advice on how to handle failure. You are not the first, or only, entrepreneur who has failed. Seeking counsel from those who failed and overcame can prove beneficial. This will help mitigate potential risk of injury to you and your family from failure.

3. *Create a support group:* Like with risks, failures cause stress, and stress causes anxiety and that can lead to mental injury. You should not underestimate the power of stress due to failure and the effects it can have on your well-being. Like with any other potentiality, you need to be prepared to handle the stress associated failure not only on yourself but also on your employees.

Success, for me, some of my goals, throughout my career were: Graduating as an engineer, building a successful team, starting my own company, running my company at a profit, becoming the best, obtaining my Professional Engineer (P.E.) certification.

The fear then, for me, was directly linked to each of those goals: Fear of not graduating, fear of not being able to build a successful team, fear of not being able to convince clients to trust me, fear of financial ruin, fear of not being good enough, fear of not obtaining my P.E. certification.

Failure, for me, then, at one point in time, followed closely behind some of my fears: I was forced to declare academic bankruptcy in my goal of graduating as an engineer; I had to build my staff and start my company during the Great Recession; I did not have the needed P.E. certification to start my own firm; I suffered numerous cash flow problems; I had many insecurities about whether I would succeed, and so on. But, I learned from each of my initial failures and pushed forward, ultimately achieving success in each of those goals, with one exception.

The following is a more detailed explanation of my life experiences with goals, fears, and failures:

1. *The goal* (graduating as an engineer): *The fear* (not graduating): *The failure* (academic bankruptcy): I almost did not attain this goal. I had failed out of school and was working odd jobs with no direction. With renewed determination, I sought out help and due to the kindness of an associate dean at the university, I was given a second chance. I declared academic bankruptcy and began my academic career anew. Through preparation and hard work, I excelled the second time around and attained my goal of earning a degree in engineering.

2. *The goal* (building a successful team): *The fear* (not being able to build a successful team): *The failure* (the Great Recession): Despite this fear, I left my first job of 13 plus years of working in the only discipline I had ever known. I took a huge pay cut and gamble and went to work for another firm outside of my area of specialty in the hopes that I could transfer my knowledge and experience and build a successful team at the new company. I had conquered that fear and achieved my goal. However, during this period, which came to be

known as the Great Recession, all engineering firms were undergoing financial hardship, and I had to make another career move. I decided to leave that firm and start my own firm.

3. *The goal* (starting my own company): *The fear* (not being able to convince clients to trust me): *The failure* (not having a P.E. certification): I had made a rash decision to leave my previous firm and start my own firm without knowing if the clients would follow me and trust me with their work. It was a difficult time in the engineering industry, due to the Great Recession, because I would be starting my firm, while other firms were struggling. On top of all of that, I did not have a P.E. certification, which was required to start an engineering company. I had taken a big gamble and risk. My solution was to hire a P.E. and make him or her my vice president and company qualifier. I would then offer our services at a reduced fee. The business model of better service at a reduced rate worked. I was able to build my company up quickly. Due to the Great Recession, there was an abundance of highly qualified engineers who had been laid off, and I was able to secure them to work for me at an affordable salary.

4. *The goal* (running my company at a profit): *The fear* (financial ruin): *The failure* (cash flow problems): After the Great Recession ended and the economy started to pick up, I lost many of those same high-qualified engineers to larger general engineering firms from which they originally came from. At one point, I lost my top three engineers within a short period of time. My revenue and cash flow suffered tremendously because I had to rebuild my company and had lost many clients due to lack of manpower. I focused, rehired, retrained used up most of my financial reserves, and got the company back on its feet.

5. *The goal* (becoming the best): *The fear* (not being good enough): *The failure* (insecurities): I always had a dream of being the best. Becoming an expert in my field. But, how could I do that, I thought, without having a P.E.? I had already become an expert in field based on experience, but I did not have the most important credential, so I thought, the certification as a professional engineer. Without that, I would just be a graduate in engineering with its corresponding degree. I became insecure, and that prevented me from seeking out expert witness status and cases. During a personal experience with

hurricane damage and losses suffered at my condo unit, as part of a suit I had filed against the insurance company for failure to adequately estimate my losses, I was exposed to experts on both sides of the case. I quickly realized that I had more knowledge than both experts had combined, in my area of expertise, which was the exterior building envelope and hurricane mitigation. I had gathered and prepared evidence that essentially disqualified the testimony and opinion provided by the opposing expert. My input and professional opinion ended up being a big reason why the insurance company agreed to settle the case to our satisfaction. At the end of my case, based on the demonstration of my knowledge in the field, I was hired by both our expert and my attorney to perform expert witness assessments on future cases.

6. *The goal* (obtaining my P.E. certification): *The fear* (not obtaining P.E. certification): *The failure* (not obtaining P.E. certification): This is the one professional goal that I am still working on and has become my cross to bear. The reason it has eluded me, to date, is both pride and my choice of specialty. My degree is in architectural engineering. When I graduated, I went to work immediately with a specialty engineering firm dedicated only to design of the exterior building envelope for hurricane mitigation. Therefore, I gained no experience in architectural engineering, which includes the design of only building structures and all its services such as mechanical, electrical, and plumbing. The P.E. exams are not designed to test your knowledge of what you learned in school, that is, the engineer in training (E.I. or F.E.) exam, which I passed on my first attempt. The P.E. exam is designed to test knowledge gained after five years of practical experience in your field. At the time of my graduation, there was no P.E. exam for architectural engineering. The only options for a P.E. included taking the civil or the structural exams. The civil exam covers design of all structures and not just buildings (transportation, highways, environmental, and so on) courses, which were not required in my degree in architectural engineering. The structural exam covers all structures and all loading conditions and not just buildings (bridges and earthquake loads, and so on). The easiest route, the route most people take, is to sit for the civil exam,

which has a much higher passing rate then the structural exam. My stubbornness forced me to focus on the structural exam, which has the lowest pass rate of all the P.E. exams including civil because it is the field most closely related to my degree. Why would I take the civil exam, which includes areas of practice and design that I never learned in school and strive to learn those concepts, essentially self-teaching myself university-level courses in transportation, highway, and environmental design, if I did not plan to work in civil engineering? Therefore, instead, I decided to take on the challenge of self-teaching myself university-level courses in bridge and earthquake design. The results were predictable. I did however manage to secure a 69 when the passing rate was 70. But as they say, close is only good when playing horseshoes and with hand grenades. Today, there is a P.E. exam for architectural engineering, but I have never practiced it due to the dedication to my area of specialty. The irony is, if I had become and architectural engineer, I probably would not have my own firm today and be considered an expert in my field. I have come to understand and determine that a P.E. is helpful to have in my field, but it is not essential to success. Nonetheless, I have not given up on this goal. I have decided to set my pride aside and learn the basics of transportation, highway, and environmental design, and so on, through online courses and retake the exam. Because of the COVID-19 pandemic, online courses are much more prevalent and accessible. I plan to take the civil engineering P.E. exam this coming April in 2021. Wish me luck.

Chapter 9: Do Not Be Afraid to Fail

Recommended Activities

1. Make a list of times you have failed in the past and include details of what you failed at and why.
2. Recall and write down how you handled it.
3. List what you learned from each of your past failures.
4. Write down your definition of happiness.
5. Write down your definition success.
6. Rethink your definition of failure based on your new definition of success. Failure is the lack of (insert your definition of success). Do this for each subgoal.

PART III

How to Practice Like an Entrepreneur

This part of the book will focus on putting your ideas to practical use. Now that you have learned how to *think* like an entrepreneur (chapters 1 through 3) and how to *act* like an entrepreneur (chapters 4 through 9), it is time to learn how to *practice* like an entrepreneur and become an entrepreneur (chapters 10 through 14).

For more information regarding the topics covered in Chapter 10 (Start a Business) and Chapter 11 (Manage and Grow Your Business) and a much more comprehensive and detailed account of how to start and manage your own firm, I highly recommend reading my book: Engineer to Entrepreneur: Success Strategies to Manage Your Career and Start Your Own Firm (e2E), starting on Chapter 6 of that book where I detail everything you need to know from: funding your start-up company (Chapter 6), company start-up logistics (Chapter 7), office start-up logistics (Chapter 8), marketing and communications (Chapter 9), and management (Chapter 10). In chapters 10 and 11 of this book, I focus more on the concept and idea of starting your own firm, as opposed to the actual step-by-step procedures, which I have already covered in e2E. In chapters 10 and 11, wherever I feel that you can derive benefit by referencing e2E, in that topic, I will include the note: "See e2E chapter x, page y". "Excerpts from Engineer to Entrepreneur © 2016 American Society of Civil Engineers used with permission of the publisher. All rights reserved."

When I speak of practicing, I am not speaking of repetition of actions to improve ability. Nor am I trying to invoke thoughts of Allen Iverson "…we talkin' 'bout practice??" (For those of you unfamiliar with the reference, Google Allen Iverson and practice). I am speaking of the art of putting what you have learned to good use or "the actual application or use of an idea, belief, or method, as opposed to theories relating to it."

In this part of the book, I will focus on the implementation of the first two parts of the book. How to think and act like and entrepreneur. How to:

1. Start a business (Chapter 10). *See also chapters 6 through 8 of e2E.*
2. Manage and grow a business (Chapter 11). *See also chapters 9 and 10 of e2E.*
3. Create and cultivate your brand (Chapter 12).
4. Give back (Chapter 13).

CHAPTER 10

Start a Business

Owning a business is not for everyone, but for those brave enough it can provide fulfillment and freedom of purpose.

This chapter will focus on the *idea, challenges, and benefits* of starting your own firm. It will provide you with a basic understanding of how to go about it. The best way that I can teach you what it takes and why to do it, including the expected challenges and benefits, is by providing you with my own personal example, which I have included at the end of the chapter.

I have written this chapter to give you a general understanding of what it takes to start a business. For a complete understanding of exactly how to start a business, I highly recommend reading my book: Engineer to Entrepreneur: Success Strategies to Manage Your Career and Start Your Own Firm (e2E), chapters 6 through 8, where I detail everything you need to know about starting a business from: funding your start-up company (Chapter 6), company start-up logistics (Chapter 7), and office start-up logistics (Chapter 8). In this chapter, wherever I feel that you can derive much benefit by referencing e2E, in that topic, I will include the note: "See e2E chapter x, page y". "Excerpts from Engineer to Entrepreneur © 2016 American Society of Civil Engineers used with permission of the publisher. All rights reserved."

Before you start a business, you need to know if you are ready. You cannot jump into entrepreneurship unprepared.

The five questions any aspiring entrepreneur should ask themselves before starting a business:

1. Do I have a specialty or niche that involves a specific idea, product, or service?

2. Is there a need and demand for the idea, product, or service I have chosen?

3. Do I have the necessary knowledge to become an expert and entrepreneur in my chosen field?
4. Can I create an efficiently trained team and staff to follow and adhere to the quality and standards that I have learned?
5. Have I established good relationships with the people I have worked with, and will they trust me with their business?

The preceding questions were posed in my first book (e2E) and were explained in much detail. I also provided examples of the answers to each based on my own experience. *See e2E, Chapter 5, page 55.*

Why should you start a business? You start a business to affect change and make a difference in society. To put your ideas to practical use. To attain financial independence. To take control of your future. To put yourself in a position to give back. To establish a legacy. To provide yourself a purposeful vehicle in which to channel your energy and passion.

What are the expected challenges you may face in starting a business? The expected challenges include fear of risk, fear of failure, financial strain, extreme time commitments, cash flow issues, pressure of responsibility, and inherent sacrifices.

What are the expected benefits you may derive in starting a business? The benefits that await you include financial flexibility and independence, control over your future, the use of a tax shelter, investment potential, and name recognition.

Once you have determined that you have the necessary preparation to start a business and the motivation, the next step is to start your business. Starting a business entails seven key steps:

The seven key steps to starting a business	
1	Come up with a good name
2	Decide on a legal business structure
3	Incorporate your business
4	Set up company policies
5	Apply for board or state certification and licenses
6	Apply for business tax receipt
7	Implement legal, taxation, and insurance requirements

1. *Come up with a good name*: Your name choice should reflect your business interest. You need to do your research and make sure you do not choose a name that infringes on another person's registered name. *See e2E, Chapter 7, page 87.*

2. *Decide on a legal business structure*: There are several business structures to choose from, all with distinct advantages, mainly: C corporation, S corporation, limited liability company, partnership, and sole proprietorship. I recommend choosing an S corporation. It provides the most protection, the same as a C corporation, but you are taxed at your personal rate, called passed through taxation, instead of the corporate rate, which can be much higher. You can declare your company losses and gains on your personal tax return using it as a potential tax shelter. *See e2E, Chapter 7, page 89.*

3. *Incorporate your business*: Incorporating your business requires you to file incorporation papers with your state; the person who files the papers is known as the incorporator. Requirements to incorporate includes the following information (requirements may vary from state to state): *see e2E, Chapter 7, page 91.*

   (a) Legal business name: Pick a unique name that does not infringe on any other business's brand or name selection. The name of your business will be affected by the legal structure you use, as it must be followed by the appropriate designation (", Inc.," ", Corp.," ", LLC," and so on).

   (b) Business address: The location where the business will be conducted.

   (c) Purpose of business: Most states allow you to put "For any legal purpose" as to not limit your options.

   (d) Number of shares: The initial number of shares is entirely up to you. It can be 100 or 1,000,000. The value of the company will be divided by the number of shares issued. The shareholders are the legal owners of the company, and their percentage of shares equals their percentage of ownership. For sole shareholders, I recommend selecting 100 shares and assigning all 100 to yourself. You can always increase or decrease the number of shares, which would then reallocate ownership percentages according to who control the shares depending on the value of your company.

(e) Board of directors and initial officers: The board of directors, headed by the chairman of the board, are the people assigned by the shareholders to oversee the company and elect the officers. The officers of the company are elected by the board of directors to run the company headed by the president. For the purposes of incorporation, only president, treasurer and secretary are required.

(f) Registered agent: This is the individual assign to be the official point of contact between the Internal Revenue Service (IRS) and the company with respect to notifications.

(g) Incorporator: This is the individual who files and submits the incorporation papers.

You should also purchase and complete your company by-laws, issue stocks, and open a bank account. Company by-laws are the rules by which the company is run and organized. It spells out the roles of officers, records the shares of stock, and contains sample company meeting minutes, resolutions, and includes the corporate seal.

4. *Set up company policies*: Company policies are the rules by which the office is run and is important to have to eliminate confusion and avoid potential liability. *See e2E, Chapter 7, page 94.*

5. *Apply for board or state certification and licenses*: For professional corporations, it may be necessary to apply for board certification from your state. *See e2E, Chapter 7, page 95.*

6. *Apply for business tax receipt*: In addition to state certification, you most likely, depending on your state, will need to apply to do business in the city and county in which your business is located. *See e2E, Chapter 7, page 96.*

7. *Implement legal, taxation, and insurance requirements*: When starting a business, you must become aware of the many legal, tax, and insurance requirements such as: *See e2E, Chapter 7, page 96.*

(a) New hire reporting: Each new employee hire must be reported to the government: https://acf.hhs.gov/css/employers/employer-responsibilities/new-hire-reporting

(b) Employment eligibility verification (I-9): This form is required to be provided to the government, for each new employee, to confirm employment eligibility: https://uscis.gov/i-9

(c) How to conduct proper interviews: Not all questions are appropriate or legal to ask of your potential employees during interview: Https://Eeoc.Gov/Overview

(d) Noncompete, confidentiality, and nondisclosure agreements: If you have employees who you train in an area of specialty, these documents help protect you from them using that knowledge to compete against you or to share proprietary information with others.

(e) Patents, trademarks, and copyrights: These documents protect you from people trying to profit from your ideas.

(f) Apply for your company's employer identification number (EIN): Most companies are required to have a unique identification number, similar to your social security number: https://ein.e-tax-filings.com/business-select-b/

(g) Apply for small business status: This status applies to corporations that want to take advantage of pass-through taxation and be recognized by the IRS as a small business corporation, S corporation: https://irs.gov/forms-instructions

(h) Understand federal, state, county, and city taxes.

(i) Understand your state corporation fees.

(j) Understand your insurance requirements: Workers compensation, general and professional liability.

Why did I decide to start a business? I did not consider becoming an entrepreneur until late in my career. This was partly because of a set of fears and partly because I was comfortable and content with where I was. I was not being paid well, but I was given lots of responsibility, and I was constantly learning. I guess it just never occurred to me. I was afraid of the unknown. I was not sure if I could run a company and take on the responsibility of being an employer. It was not until I hit a rough patch in my life, coupled with hitting a ceiling at work, after many years, that I started to seriously consider it. I had just gotten divorced, and my job was no longer fulfilling to me. I was stuck doing very tedious work that I did not find challenging. I was not learning anymore. I had become stagnant. I found myself looking at my watch every day hoping that it was time to go home. Finally, I got the courage to make a dramatic change in my life. I decided, after 13 years, to leave the only place I had ever known as a professional. It almost felt like if I was leaving home again. It was a terrifying decision. I could no longer hide from my fears, so I decided to confront them head on. Instead of taking comfort by going to work for another company that did something similar, a job that would allow for a smooth transition, I decided to take a totally different path. I decided to do something that I was ill-prepared to do. I decided to go work for a firm that did only general structural engineering. I left my comfort zone. I decided to leave the field of engineering in which I had practiced for so many years. A specialty that was the only thing I knew how to do. I was embarking on something totally foreign to me. I thought to myself, how will I ever get hired to do general structural engineering when I had never practiced it, and I was in my 40s? I figured I would learn something new, but how would I sell myself? So, I decided to make a bold decision. I asked to be paid entry level. It would mean a drastic pay cut. However, there would be a catch. The agreement was that I was to be paid entry level for the first year, with the understanding that my compensation would be adjusted at the end of the year if I was able to originate enough work in my field. The deal was that if I did bring in the work, I would be brought on par with what I had made the year before at my previous company. We had a deal. I was the first one to work the next day. I had a renewed sense of excitement mixed in with some trepidation. Could I learn to do the general structural work? Would I be able to bring in work in my field? I had asked for a little time to get the staff trained and ready in case I could bring in the work. In the meantime, I would do whatever they asked me to do until I was ready. As it turns out, I did not get a chance to do too much general structural work because I had severely underestimated myself. I got to work on some foundations and some structural repair inspections for a few months until word got out that I had left my job and had gone to work for another firm. Some of the people I had done work for had found out where I had gone and tracked me down. They asked if I was willing to do some work for them. I was not ready, but I could not say no. After all, this was my field of specialty, and I knew the work backward and forward. I would do all the work myself and train the staff on the fly. Soon, more and more work in my specialty started pouring in without a single phone call or marketing on my part. You see, as it turns out, it appears that I did good work, and the clients took notice, and some followed. I worked at the new firm for three years. Most of the time was spent overloaded with work and asking for more help so I could go out and bring in more. The economy was experiencing a bad downturn, and my requests for assistance went unheeded. Nonetheless, after my first year, I had generated considerable work for the firm and was compensated as agreed. My next review did not go so well even though I continued to generate a lot of work for the company. But, I decided to stick it out a little longer. I had managed to take a new discipline into a company that had no experience in that field, train the staff to work in that field, and bring in work, but the economy was in a tailspin. It became apparent that I had quickly hit another ceiling at my new job. I became disillusioned. It was time to make another move. I kept expressing my disappointment with my current situation to my wife (I had since remarried) who by now had grown tired of hearing me complain. One night, I must have been complaining a little too much and she finally said...just shut up and do it. I do not recall if she said it quite that way, but it sure felt like it because it certainly made an impression on me. So, I decided to quit my job and go into business for myself. I was told by my current employer that it was a bad time to quit my job due to the economic downturn. I was advised to take some time and think about my decision, but my mind was made up, and I gave immediate notice of my intent to resign. I was going to enter the entrepreneurial field in engineering during a time when existing firms were laying people off and downsizing due to the poor economy. But, I had a plan. I would offer equal or better quality of service at a reduced rate. It made sense, as, at my current job, I had built up a following of old contacts and generated new business based on my knowledge and experience. The people I had worked with in the past followed me to my new place of employment; why would they not follow me yet again? I would assure them that on my own, I would be in a position to offer them better rates, more flexibility in terms, and better service, as I would be the one making all the decisions, not having to rely on someone else to set the terms and fees. I had quit my job, used my life's savings, along with financial support from my wife, to set up my company out of our home. DLG Engineering was born.

What are the challenges that I faced in starting my own firm? The biggest challenge I faced was overcoming the fear of failure. Could I train a staff to uphold my standards of quality, and would clients trust me with their work? This fear caused me to prepare and plan. In my case, the fear was assuaged a bit when I left my first job of 13 plus years to a new firm that practiced a totally different discipline. It was like starting my own firm, but without the financial responsibly. No one in the firm knew the specialty of which I was bringing in, so I had to train the staff to perform the tasks and supervise them to make sure the quality of work was up to par. Sure enough, my preparation paid off, and I was able to train a staff, and the clients followed. There was still a lot at risk such as my reputation and my salary because I made an arrangement where I took a huge pay cut when I was first hired, with the understanding that if I could originate work for the company based on my area of specialty, that I would then be compensated accordingly. Once I decided to leave that company and start my own firm, the fear returned. This time it was a fear of being financially responsible for not only myself, but for my employees. There was also the fear of: would the clients follow me if I set up a new company with no history of success? Once again, I prepared and had a plan. I would offer equal or better service for a lesser fee. It worked. Once you open your own company, the challenges turn to other areas. Highest among them is cash flow management and meeting your financial liabilities. Choosing the right staff. The financial hurdle for me of finding start-up funding was not that big of a concern because I had implemented the strategy and use of my 401K and equity in my homes as start-up funding and had managed to reduce my liabilities and expenses in preparation.

What are the benefits that I have derived from starting my own company? The benefits I have derived from starting and owning my own company and being an entrepreneur are almost too many to list. It has been entirely worth all the sacrifices that I have made. Having done it with a management style that requires less day-to-day management than most business owners, it has allowed me to pursue other endeavors and interests. Endeavors such as being an expert witness, peer reviewer, and investing in real estate. Interests such as freedom to travel, to write a book, or two, the ability to pursue my passion in photography, and an opportunity to be actively involved in the community. None of these would have been possible, or at the very least it would have been much more difficult, if I had a 9 to 5 job. Other benefits that I have derived include the freedom to choose the projects I work on and the number of interesting people I have met. It has provided me a seat at the table, with much larger and universally recognized firms because of my unique area of specialty. It has provided me the opportunity to demonstrate my expertise though all sorts of media and give back to the community. It has given me financial flexibility and freedom. It has given me a sense of purpose and an identity. Without a doubt, opening my own company and, more specifically, becoming an entrepreneur has been the best business decision of my life.

Chapter 10: Start a Business

Recommended Activities

1. Read chapters 6 through 8 of *Engineer to Entrepreneur: Success Strategies to Manage Your Career and Start your Own Firm.*
2. Come up with a good name.
3. Decide on a legal business structure.
4. Incorporate your business.
5. Set up company policies.
6. Apply for board or state certification and licenses.
7. Apply for business tax receipt.
8. Implement legal, taxation, and insurance requirements.

CHAPTER 11

Manage and Grow
Your Business

Management is the oil that keeps the company engine running smooth.

This chapter will focus on the *idea and concept* of effectively managing and growing your company. It will provide you with a basic understanding of how to go about it. The best way that I can teach you how to manage and grow your business is by providing you with my own personal example, which I have included in each section and at the end of the chapter.

I have written this chapter to give you a general understanding of what it takes to manage and grow your business. For a complete understanding of exactly how to manage and grow a business, I highly recommend reading my book: "Engineer to Entrepreneur: Success Strategies to Manage Your Career and Start Your Own Firm" (e2E), chapters 9 and 10, where I detail everything you need to know about managing and growing a business from marketing and communications (Chapter 9) to management (Chapter 10). In this chapter, wherever I feel that you can derive benefit by referencing e2E, in that topic, I will include the note: "See e2E chapter x, page y". "Excerpts from Engineer to Entrepreneur © 2016 American Society of Civil Engineers used with permission of the publisher. All rights reserved."

Effective management encompasses many aspects within a company, all of which are essential to success. Like a chain, the strength of a company may be limited by the strength of any given link at any given time. To have a strong and successful company, your chain must be strong. Every link must support and transfer its own load to the next link to move or support an object. In the case of a company, the object you are trying to move, or support, is success. To effectively manage your business, you must understand the eight key areas of company management:

The eight key areas of company management	
1	Office
2	Cash flow
3	Client
4	Project
5	Employee
6	Payroll
7	Contract worker
8	Profit

1. *Office*: Running the office efficiently and establishing clear office policies are critical for the success of the company. It involves properly
   handling the office business accounts, vendor accounts and contracts,
   professional association membership, professional and occupational
   licenses, online accounts and passwords, inventory of office equipment and warranties, copies of insurance policies, employee files,
   company records and accounting reports, Internal Revenue Service
   (IRS) quarterly reports, profit and loss reports, balance sheet reports,
   payroll reports, and aging reports. In my case, I selected, trained, and
   delegated authority to three key individuals: my vice president, an
   office manager, and a project manager. I trained them to utilize the
   tools that I have created to provide excellent service to our clients.
   Information that includes all aspects of running a successful office.
   I defer to my office manager. I get involved only if an issue arises,
   and I judge success based on employee and vendor satisfaction. I do
   not get involved in the day-to-day office management. I delegate and
   trust, but verify. *See e2E, Chapter 10, page 138.*

2. *Cash flow*: Learning to manage cash flow is the most important
   financial aspect of a successful company. It includes invoicing, aging
   reports, payment incentives, and collections. Keeping a steady cash
   flow is the only way to meet your business liabilities and expenses.
   In my case, I track and manage the cash flow by constantly reviewing the available financial reports such as the aging reports through
   the QuickBooks accounting software and the jobs under contract
   spreadsheet, which I created myself to track all the status of all committed revenue. This information allows me to make informed deci-

sions to make sure the cash flow runs smoothly. *See e2E Chapter 10, page 142.*

3. *Client:* Understanding all the different client personalities and knowing who your most valuable clients are is critical to job growth and client relations. You must ask yourself the following questions: Is the client a repeat or loyal client? Does the client pay in a timely manner? Is the client demanding and constantly pushing deadlines? Does the client ask for services not in the original scope of work? Does the client refer work to you? Is the client high profile? In my case, I have learned to identify all the different client types and I act accordingly. *See e2E, Chapter 10, page 144.*

4. *Project:* Properly identifying the exact type and scope of work and proper handling of your workload can save you potential misunderstandings with your clients. At job origination you should: identify and explain potential hurdles, detail the exact scope of work, identify services that are considered additional services not included in fee, identify exclusions from the scope of work, exact proposal terms and conditions, fee and payment terms, and estimated project completion date. In my case I defer to my project manager. I get involved only if an issue arises, and I judge success based on client satisfaction and cash flow. I have developed spreadsheets to keep track of all project-related information to gage success, including review of individual project profitability. *See e2E, Chapter 10, page 145.*

5. *Employee:* Hiring, evaluating, managing, and firing employees is key to maintaining company chemistry to ensure a good working environment for all and to establish quality control. Important items to consider and track include: the initial interview, date of hire, initial pay rate, yearly evaluations, confirmation as to understanding of office policies, explanation of company benefits, date of promotions or increases, and date of termination or resignation. In my case, I make it a point to make sure the employees I hire have good chemistry and are versatile. I empower my vice president with input. *See e2E, Chapter 10, page 148.*

6. *Payroll:* Making sure you understand all tax implications and can meet your payroll liabilities is one of the more complex parts of owning your own firm. It includes taxes (federal and state employer

corporate income, federal and state employee income, federal employer and employee Social Security and Medicare, employer federal and state unemployment), bonuses, paid time-off, overtime pay, retirement benefits, and insurance benefits. In my case, I always review the payroll and sign the checks as well as track the invoicing, collections, and cash flow to ensure the company meets its payroll liabilities. *See e2E, Chapter 10, page 150.*

7. Contract worker: Properly utilizing 1099 contractors can help reduce company overhead if done in accordance with the guidelines of the IRS. The typical guidelines of whether an individual qualifies to be paid as a contract worker include the answers to the following questions: Can they set their own hours? Can they work from home? Can they hire people to assist them in their tasks? Can they set their own fee? Do they provide your company with invoices for services rendered? It is important to request the contract workers social security numbers, for issuance of a 1099 statement, and save their invoices. In my case I, try and hire 1099 contract workers for specific tasks to lighten the burden on payroll taxes and benefits. *See e2E, Chapter 10, page 154.*

8. Profit: Learning to properly determine actual profit is important to understand if the company goals are being attained. This is done by tracking: overhead, using a multiplier analysis to set rates and fees, determining your fee structure, understanding when to charge a flat fee, learning to utilize additional services, and learning to manage profit to take advantage of available tax shelters. In my case, I have a unique approach to taking profit. I prefer to use the profit that the company makes and reinvest it at the end of the year back into my company. I do this in the form of employee bonuses, purchases of new equipment, paying down of liabilities and expenses, and so on. What this accomplishes is to strengthen my company while lessening my tax burden. I can do this because I am the sole shareholder and the only owner of the company. If not, I would have a fiduciary responsibility to the other shareholders to realize that profit. *See e2E, Chapter 10, page 156.*

Once you learn how to effectively manage your company, you need to learn to grow it. This is done by thorough marketing and communications as well as networking and originating. This is where I get heavily involved. I rarely delegate these tasks. As I am the brand of my company, I make the sales pitches. Once the client is secured, I hand them off to my project managers.

Marketing and communications: Marketing and communications are key to growing your company. Marketing is more externally focused, whereas communications is both externally and internally focused. In order to grow your company, you must be able to find clients and convince them that you are the best option they have and why they should select your product or service over that of your competitors. To grow your company, you must be able to communicate effectively internally to improve your services and externally to relay the right message.

Marketing: Marketing is defined as "activities undertaken by a company to promote the buying or selling of a product or service." This is best done by:

1. Creating credentials and self-promotion: Credentials set you apart and, by definition, provide credibility. As an entrepreneur, you are the brand and identity of your company, you must actively promote yourself as an expert in your field. *See e2E, Chapter 9, page 116.*

2. Company and name recognition: Opportunities for recognition for your company and for yourself will not always present themselves. You must actively seek them out. Putting your company name and your own out there to be recognized for what you do is the first step to success. *See e2E, Chapter 9, page 117.*

3. Establishing a marketing strategy: You cannot just advertise your company, your product, and your services, to just anyone. If you want to achieve success, you must develop a detailed and comprehensive plan based on research and understanding of the market. You must understand what people want and what people need, and the difference between the two. What people want (a desire) is quite often a luxury, for them, and may be subject to, and limited by, their

means, priorities, trends, and the economy. What people need (a necessity) is fundamental to them and may not be limited by their means and will be prioritized highly and less dependent of trends or the economy. People will, quite often, exceed their means for, or prioritize highly, something they need. It is okay to target both, but you must understand the limitations and differences between the two. Your company should have a good balance, of services and/or products, targeted between wants and needs and not rely only, or too heavily, on addressing wants, if you want to be insulated from changing trends or a bad economy. You should try to prioritize identifying needs and focus on a market, with those needs, with a means (product or service) to address those needs. *See e2E, Chapter 9, page 119.*

4. Joining professional associations: The best way to get your name out there is to associate and surround yourself with people in your profession. *See e2E, Chapter 9, page 121.*

5. Building an effective website: While there are many forms of marketing available today because of social media, having a good website is still considered a sign of credibility. *See e2E, Chapter 9, page 125.*

6. Utilizing proper marketing materials: Aside from social media, the traditional form of advertising your services, such as creating effective flyers and brochures, is still productive, especially for face-to-face meetings. *See e2E, Chapter 9, page 127.*

7. Word-of-mouth advertising: The best form of marketing and advertising is having performed well for a previous client and getting their endorsement. *See e2E, Chapter 9, page 127.*

Communications: Communications is defined as "the imparting or exchanging of information or news." This is best done by:

1. Internal communications:
   (a) Staff meetings: Before you can communicate effectively with your clients, you must be able to communicate effectively with your staff. *See e2E, Chapter 9, page 129.*
   (b) Staff evaluations: To provide the best possible service to your clients, you must first assemble a good staff. *See e2E, Chapter 9, page 130.*

(c) Staff motivation: Once you find a good staff, you need to make sure you address their needs to ensure continuity. *See e2E, Chapter 9, page 130.*

(d) Office policies: Having clear office policies and making your staff aware of them is essential to avoiding misunderstandings. *See e2E, Chapter 9, page 131.*

2. External communications:

(a) Online media: Sharing company information with the public on social media can help bring awareness to your company in ways you never would otherwise assume. *See e2E, Chapter 9, page 132.*

(b) Newsletters: Keeping your clients informed of the latest trends promotes loyalty. *See e2E, Chapter 9, page 133.*

(c) Sales pitch: The best way to originate work is to have a good sales pitch and learn to deliver it with confidence. *See e2E, Chapter 9, page 133.*

(d) Presentations: The best ways to close a deal is with a good, concise, and well-thought-out presentation. *See e2E, Chapter 9, page 134.*

(e) E-mails: The best form of communication, aside from making a phone call, is via an e-mail. E-mails allow you to have conversations on the record and avoid disputes or misunderstanding. Important conversations should be followed up with a concise e-mail detailing what was agreed. *See e2E, Chapter 9, page 134.*

Networking: Networking is defined as "the action or process of interacting with others to exchange information and develop professional or social contacts." Networking is not standing around with a drink in your hand with your friends or co-workers as you scan the crowd, as I have quite often noticed. Real networking consists of:

1. *Identifying the right targets for face-to-face encounters*: Knowing where to network and with whom to network is the first step in successful networking. Target venues that will include people who directly, or indirectly, provide or refer business to you. That is an important point. You never know where work can originate from and who is

listening to your pitch. When it comes to who to target, the best source are the people you have been working with for most of your life. These people, provided you have dealt honestly and dependably with them, are your best source of potential start-up clients. Build a rapport, and do not lose touch with them throughout their careers. Also, do not only look to target those individuals who can directly use your services, but rather target, as well, individuals who are in position to recommend those people to use your services. Good venue areas and types to target for good networking opportunities include professional association meetings or events (seek work or collaboration among your peers), alumni association group events (utilize common bonds to generate leads), professional annual conferences (target specialized individuals that can refer work to you), and local lunch and learn or continuing education sessions (attend a session that closely resembles your specialty and develop relationships). Do not discount networking at social functions that are frequented by potential clients.

2. *Utilizing online tools and social media*: The best online platform for professional networking is LinkedIn. But, like any other media, you need to invest in it to derive a benefit. Investing is not opening it up and reading the articles and posts and then reaching out for connections that you then aggressively target for work. I am put off by connections that I accept only to receive within minutes a solicitation for work. Like with face-to-face networking, it is all about building a relationship. Finding common ground and common interests first. The first step is to make sure your profile is complete and includes all pertinent, and updated, information on your experiences, qualifications, projects, accomplishments, and recognitions. The next step is to understand the proper way to invest in LinkedIn to derive a benefit from it. That is to actively participate. Write an article and post it. Use the hashtag options with keywords to help attract your target audience. Do not just like, but also comment on other people's posts. You would be surprised to know what a simple *good job* comment on a post can derive (a visit to your page, a personal response) versus just a *like*. Join a like-minded group and participate in their discussions. Create a group and invite like-minded individuals.

Many people look down on social media sites such as Facebook and neglect it all together. That would be a mistake. Why discount free advertising? You never know who is watching your feed or page. It could be a friend of a friend who might need your services. However, unlike LinkedIn, where the venue is strictly professional, this venue is primarily social. Therefore, if you are going to befriend potential clients and professional contacts, be very mindful of what you post. A way to keep your personal life separate is to create a Facebook business page.

3. *Building relationships*: Effective networking is about building relationships. I have found that in your face, hard sales pitch's turns people off. Some people just sense a sales pitch coming and close up. You must get to know your target at a personal level first. Talk to them about themselves and their projects first. Successful people love to talk about themselves. When they feel comfortable with you and see that you are interested in them and not just their business, they will relax and open up. Find something in common (sports team, school, family experiences, projects) and start building a bond. You may not even make your pitch until sometime in the future, but you are planting a seed and building a rapport. Cultivate and nurture the relationship. Then you introduce a mutually beneficial proposal.

4. *Providing collaborative and mutually beneficial associations:* Once you identify the right target, have built a rapport, and are getting ready to make your sales pitch, take time to consider how you can make the professional relationship mutually beneficial. Some of the ways to do that include offering them a savings from their current expenses in your scope of work, providing better-quality services that can increase their productivity, providing faster response times to make their office more efficient, or referring business to them. The most successful, and longest lasting, relationships are those in which both sides are benefactors and beneficiaries.

Originating: Originating is defined as to "create or initiate something." In the case of entrepreneurs, the focus is on originating business by initiating relationships. Networking and originating go hand in hand. For the purposes of this chapter, we will consider networking as bringing the client to the table, whereas originating, we will consider closing the deal. Learning to originate business requires:

1. Identification of your target clients: For originating business, from the results of your networking efforts, you should focus, from the list of potential clients, on potential repeat clients or clients of value such as those who can bring exposure to your firm or include you in iconic projects. See also networking described earlier.

2. A great sales pitch: There is no substitute for face-to-face meetings to close a deal, even if it is via video conference due to the social distancing limitations that occurred due to the COVID-19 global pandemic. Being able to read your target's facial expressions and mannerisms to your pitch and being able to adapt and improvise can be the difference in securing that contract. That involves emotional intelligence. Be advised, however, that no amount of emotional intelligence can save you from a bad presentation. You need to be prepared to pitch. Know the information and practice the meeting in your mind over and over, each time introducing the most unexpected reactions and questions from your target, and let it play out in your head of how you would react and respond. Mental simulations are extremely helpful and create a form of experience in your mind without having gone though it that can allow you to prepare for almost all contingencies. Like pilots training on flight simulations, it creates muscle and mental memory that can be useful when the actual encounter takes place.

3. A good strategy that provides value: You must back up the sales pitch with examples or information of how you have helped clients in similar situations in the past. Be prepared to provide those examples. You must also give a detailed step-by-step process and outline of how you will do the same for them. Make clear to them what the value to them will be.

4. Providing incentives. Offering a discount, or a sliding scale fee structure in exchange for bulk work, is one way to incentivize securing continued work from a client and potentially pushing them over the edge to close the deal.

I have a unique management style. I delegate, trust, but verify. I manage remotely, rarely visit the office, but review and supervise extensively. This experience came in handy when some offices were forced closed due to the COVID-19 global pandemic. However, prior to the pandemic, I trusted my office manager to run the office, my project manager to manage the projects, and my vice president to run the company. It allowed me freedom and flexibility to pursue other profitable ventures and enjoy leisure time. However, I must emphasize that this form of management style must be developed over time and planned and tweaked until you find the right mixture of leader and staff. It is a style that every entrepreneur should strive to achieve. It frees you up to pursue additional profitable ventures or investments, while still having a well-functioning one that is providing you resources that will enable you to do so. Start another company, set it up, train, delegate, and move on to the next venture and so forth.

In my case, the foundation for originating work and growing my business came from past relationships and the trust, honesty, and reliability I had fostered with people I worked with in my career. Those are the same people who followed me from my first job to my second job and eventually became clients of my firm. I took much care in developing my name recognition and brand and identity and creating credentials that it makes closing a deal much easier. I have set myself far apart from my competitors, many of which focus only on their business and the financial bottom line who are business owners, but not entrepreneurs. In summary, I grew my business through creating and cultivating my brand and developing and nurturing relationships. By understanding the differences between one-time clients and repeat clients and by providing value and experience while incentivizing potential new clients to trust me with their work in face-to-face meetings.

Just because you own a business, that alone does not make you an entrepreneur, and you do not have to own your own business to be an entrepreneur and utilize entrepreneurial skills to achieve success. As explained in Chapter 4 (Identify and Attain Your Goals), everyone's definition of success is different, and if your definition does not include owning a business, that is fine. There is no wrong answer to your definition of success.

However, you can still utilize and benefit from the entrepreneurial mindset, skills, and concepts to climb up the corporate ladder and make yourself more marketable to your firm. Thinking, acting, and practicing like an entrepreneur do not have to be limited to entrepreneurs. You can achieve this by:

1. *Networking for relationships*: Promote your company to potential clients or new recruits. Present or write an article in your field and ask your company to sponsor it. Raise awareness of your company on social media. Represent your company at job fairs.
2. *Looking for innovations*: Find ways to improve the products, services, or processes in your company, how to do things faster, better, or cheaper.
3. *Adding to the company's growth potential*: Continue your personal growth and education. Attain credentials. Mentor younger associates. Take advantage of your company's management training programs.
4. *Originating business*: Learn to pitch on behalf of your company. Set up origination meetings with potential clients with you superiors. Get to know your team and promote their services.

Surviving during a tough economy or crisis: All good entrepreneurs should know, or should learn, how to anticipate and have a plan in place to account for unexpected financial hardships or an economic or market crisis that may affect their business. They must learn to adapt to changing or challenging times or risk losing everything. At no other time in our nation's history was this scenario tested and more evident than during the 2020 COVID-19 global pandemic. The global pandemic resulted in the near-complete shutdown or lockdown of our nation's economy where no business remained unaffected. Businesses that did not, or could not, adapt were forced to close or lay off employees. As a result, the global pandemic of 2020 forever changed the way companies do business. The pandemic and subsequent economic crisis exposed company weaknesses and tested contingency plans. In my case, I sensed that I needed to have a contingency plan in place before the lockdowns began. Our engineering firm was well prepared, we created a plan, we executed it, and managed to survive when many did not. We accomplished this by:

1. Instituting a plan and process, for the office, to ensure a clean and safe working environment for the staff in the early stages of the pandemic.
2. Advising our staff of the social distance rules and regulations recommended by the Centers for Disease Control and Prevention (CDC) if the need arose to travel offsite.
3. Backing up our server and local computer hard drives and uploading all project files to a cloud service.
4. Setting up a plan for the staff to effectively work from home by utilizing their office workstation computers and monitors.
5. Exploring and utilizing virtual meeting capabilities versus face-to-face meetings for staff and clients.
6. Reviewing our revenue projections versus expenses, taking into consideration the effects from the forced closures and social distancing rules in effect.
7. Offering incentives or early payment discounts for outstanding invoices to drive up cash flow and reserve.
8. Considering the effects on our staff of decrease revenue and possible cut back of time for hourly employees.
9. Reaching out to our clients to let them know that we had a plan to effectively continue to work on their projects and how that plan may affect them.
10. Exploring and utilizing verified e-signature software to avoid having to print hardcopies of drawings and plans.
11. Setting up credit cards, wire transfer, or online payment methods to include payroll delivery.
12. Communicating with our vendors to understand their limitations and adapt as required.
13. Discussing the ramifications of the closures and potential work slowdown or shutdown with our staff and explaining our plan.
14. Consulting with our office landlord regarding their plan to handle the crisis.
15. Reducing and/or eliminating all nonessential expenses.

16. Exploring and applying for available Small Business Administration (SBA) hardship loans.
17. Terminating our month to month office lease and transitioning to 100 percent remote work. We calculated, after determining that our staff could effectively and efficiently work from home, that our company could realize a considerable financial savings. Savings for both the company and the staff that include savings of rent, utilities, parking, travel time, office attire, fuel, maintenance on vehicles, and so on.

Having an effective plan in place, with enough lead time, prior to the forced lockdown bought us the necessary time needed to effectuate a smooth transition without any interruption in service to our clients and our staff. The preceding plan can be a useful example and a good lesson on how to adapt to an economic crisis or tough economic times. The plan that we implemented worked out so well that we decided to shift our practice to a permanent work from home and shared workspace combination where we can reduce expenses without sacrificing productivity. As a business owner and entrepreneur, during unprecedented and challenging times, the health (financial and physical) and safety of your clients and staff should be paramount. As a leader, you owe it to them to be thoughtful and meticulous and put in place a good contingency plan to handle any eventuality that could affect your business. Some of the steps taken during the pandemic to mitigate the effects of the economic crisis can be applied to all general economic hardships, such as:

1. Setting up a plan for the staff to effectively work from home to save on rent and other expenses.
2. Reviewing revenue projections versus expenses and setting aside a cash or liquid asset reserve.
3. Offering incentives or early payment discounts for outstanding invoices to drive up cash flow.
4. Considering the effects on staff of decrease revenue and possible cut back of time for hourly employees.
5. Understanding the available business hardship resources.
6. Reducing or eliminating all nonessential expenses.

7. Utilizing entry-level, interns, or 1099 contractors to increase work profitability.

8. Offering discount prices to current and potential new clients in exchange for bulk work.

9. Offering uncomplicated basic services that can be handled by interns or trainees that can serve as a constant source of revenue.

10. Identifying ways to expand your scope of services within your area of expertise to compensate for lost sources of income elsewhere.

Chapter 11: Manage and Grow Your Business

Recommended Activities

1. Read chapters 9 and 10 of *Engineer to Entrepreneur: Success Strategies to Manage Your Career and Start Your Own Firm.*
2. Take a course on business management and accounting.
3. Practice your public speaking and sales pitch.
4. Identify organizations to network with.
5. Review the car analogy in Chapter 2 (What do Entrepreneurs Think About?) on the top five things entrepreneurs think about that affect their business.
6. Formulate a good contingency plan for how to survive and mitigate economic hardships and write it down.

CHAPTER 12

Create and Cultivate Your Brand

Credentials create credibility, credibility demands respect and respect afford opportunities. Build your brand around credentials.

This chapter will focus on your brand and will teach you how to create and cultivate that brand to make a name for yourself. As you will notice in the next chapter on giving back, the processes of creating a brand and giving back are intertwined. You must understand that when you are an entrepreneur, you are the brand. Would you trust a business if their owner is not trustworthy, insensitive, rude, or unreliable? Be mindful that you are the clearest representation of your company, and you must behave and act accordingly.

There is no room in branding for shyness or lack of clarity. Engage people and organizations in a positive way. Share your work. The benefit to good branding is publicity, name recognition, job origination, expert designation, increased networking opportunities, and credibility.

First, you to need to create your brand. How do you create and cultivate your brand? Establish what you want to be known for. This can be accomplished by pursing the following steps. The five steps to create your brand:

The five steps to create your brand	
1	Find your identity
2	Find your specialty
3	Become an expert
4	Create credentials
5	Become a mentor

1. *Find your identity*: Like with defining success, only you can determine your identity. You must identify what defines you and what you want to be known for and build your brand around that. Be specific and clear and work toward that goal. In my case, I found my identity by chance and only began to develop it after I started my own company. Prior to that, I did not engage in creating nor cultivating my brand. However, when I did finally understand what I wanted to be known for, I aggressively began to cultivate it. I became known as an expert in hurricane mitigation of exterior building products.

2. *Find your specialty:* Once you have identified what you want to be known for, you must choose your area of specialty. The area of practice that you will be known for and develop expertise in. In my case, my specialty found me. I became involved in, and came to know of, my specialty by accident. This happened when I applied for a job as a clerk, while at the university, at a small specialty engineering firm. Little did I know that that one decision would lead to all this. I was open-minded to an opportunity that presented itself, and I took full advantage. My specialty came to be hazard mitigation of the building envelope.

3. *Become an expert*: After you have identified your area of specialty, you need to do whatever it takes to become an expert in the field. This can be done by following the steps to cultivate your brand listed next. In my case, I trained under an expert for over 13 years and learned all there was to know about the field. I even found ways to improve upon what I had learned. Once I started my own firm, I then started to develop my identity and cultivate my brand using all the strategies listed in the next section on how to cultivate your brand.

4. *Create credentials*: In the process of becoming an expert, you need to start earning credibility. This can be accomplished by sharing your knowledge with the community and your profession in a manner that creates a name for yourself and allows you to achieve recognition. Examples of credentials are leading a professional organization, writing a book or article in your profession, achieving certifications or additional areas of specialty. In my case, once again, I did not partake in creating credentials for myself until I started my own firm. However, when I finally realized that it would be beneficial to find

ways to set myself apart from my competition, I began to find ways to increase my name recognition. I accomplished this by publishing magazine articles in my industry, heading a professional organization, writing a book, presenting papers at conferences, serving as an expert witness, being quoted in industry magazines regarding current events in my field, raising awareness of my profession by whatever means I found available.

5. *Become a mentor*: When you become a mentor, you achieve one of the highest levels of success. You get the opportunity to teach others and be able to mold and shape their careers. In my case, I have found this to be one of the most rewarding aspects of cultivating a brand for myself. Becoming known for someone who gives back and helps the profession by mentoring students or young professionals.

Second, you need to cultivate your brand, implement a plan, and get the word out and become an expert. This can be accomplished by the following: The four steps to becoming an expert:

The four steps to becoming an expert	
1	Build your identity
2	Seek recognition
3	Share your work
4	Write a book

1. *Build your identity*: Once you have identified your identity, what you want to be known for, then you must build on that identity. Create a persona around your identity. This is done through self-promotion. Frame your image around what you want to be known for professionally. Get the word out on your website, magazines, social media, and professional networking sites about what you are working on and what you want to be known for. In my case, I have found it very helpful to post on professional networking sites such as LinkedIn and even Facebook about all my events, and I always make it a point to include keywords that let people know what I want to be known for. For me, I have broken it down to two key phrases, they are hur-

ricane mitigation expert and author and entrepreneur. You would be surprised how much word gets out to individuals who do not participate, like, post, or rely on social media. I cannot tally how many people, that I do not even know, have come up to me at networking events or even social functions and mention or congratulate me on my accomplishments simply by me posting about it on social media.

2. *Seek recognition*: Become active in your professional organizations or associations. Most offer yearly awards and recognition. You need to seek out those opportunities, get the word out about what you are working on, and apply to be considered for the award or recognition. In my case, I was awarded as one of the top 100 minority-owned businesses in South simply by attending an event with my wife and applying for consideration. Had I not applied, I would not have been considered nor would I have received the recognition.

3. *Share your work*: Share you work with your community and profession. This is the best way to reach the maximum number of people. This can be done by:

   (a) *Writing an article*: Reach out to magazine editors of your professional trade publications and submit a proposal for an article. In my case, I was approached, via LinkedIn, after posting about my endeavors to raise awareness of hurricane mitigation after a series of hurricanes threatened Florida. Once I wrote the first article, that same editor reached out to me numerous other times and recommended me to other editors for stories or contributions.

   (b) *Preparing a webinar*: This is one way to put in effort once, on a presentation, in preparing the webinar, that can then be easily repeated often with little additional effort and garner much reward. In my case, I started presenting webinars when asked to do so as part of my membership in the Architectural Engineering Institute's curtain wall committee. Once I prepared the first one, presenting them again became a simple task, and I was paid a royalty for each live presentation as well as for purchases of the taped versions.

   (c) *Presenting at a conference*: This is the best way to reach out to and get feedback and learn from your peers. This will expose you to increased scrutiny of your work and provide credibility. In my case, I was asked, as part of my membership in a professional committee, to answer a call for papers to be presented at the next national conference. My abstract was approved, and I was able to present in front of my peers for the first time, increasing my brand awareness and name recognition.

(d) *Taping a podcast*: This is the best way to get word out quickly and share your expertise on current events happening that affect your profession. This can afford you the most exposure. In my case, once again, based on my postings on LinkedIn and Facebook, I was approached on two instances to tape a podcast to get my professional opinion after recent hurricanes had made landfall in the United States and the nearby island of Puerto Rico. One was a radio show podcast for Univision on the effects on the island of Puerto Rico, and the other, a more general member services podcast for an engineering career center on preparing for powerful storms. This provided me with increased exposure and credibility as an expert. I was also recently featured on a special report story on television for a Spanish language network, Telemundo, during their sweep's week on the potential effects of a powerful storm hitting the area of North Florida, an area not known for its code enforcement. The story was well received and provided me with additional credibility. I have also taped several podcasts on entrepreneurship to develop my reputation in that area as a credible source.

(e) *Presenting at a lunch and learn*: This is the best way to reach out to potential clients, as they gather in numbers to focus on what you have to say. Provide valuable information, not too much, but just a taste; demonstrate your knowledge in the field; and use that as your selling point. In my case, while I was marketing my services to potential clients and building envelope product manufacturers, I had proposed to them that I present on a workshop at their offices to educate their customers and potential customers on the hazards and proper design to mitigate hurricane damage. One such client recommended I speak at a lunch and learn that one of his suppliers attends frequently, so I did. It was extraordinarily successful, and I came away with two repeat clients based on that presentation alone plus additional work from an existing client that I had invited to attend.

4. *Write a book*: If you are an expert in your field, there should be no shortage of topics that could benefit students or professionals striving and aspiring to succeed in your profession. In my case, I was inspired by members of a professional organization after I was asked to present to their local student chapter on how I transitioned from an engineer to an entrepreneur. The success of that presentation along with many more after that was the genesis for deciding to write my first book. The success of that book, and the satisfaction derived from that experience, was the motivation to write this one. A word of caution to aspiring authors on publishing options (other than self-publishing) based on my personal experiences of trying to get my books published:

(a) Vanity press: Called such because they prey on the author's desire to see their work published. They will praise your book as excellent, but they will publish pretty much anything without even reading it and ask the author to pay for everything. They will not promote or market your book. They do not care about your online presence or marketing potential. They make their money off the authors fees, which are inflated fees charged to the authors to get their book published.

(b) Copublishing or hybrid or emerging authors: The author and publisher split the costs of publication. They may read your work and offer advice, but the author will be asked to pay a significant portion of the publishing costs. They will do as little marketing as possible. They require you to have a significant online presence and marketing potential. They make their money off the author's fees and royalties on book sales.

(c) Subsidy: They will read and critique your work. They will publish only work they deem of quality. They will offer or require the author to pay for *services* to improve the quality and sales of your book. They require you to have a significant online presence and marketing potential. They make their money off the author's fees to edit, market, and promote your book and on royalties on book sales.

(d) Traditional: They will thoroughly read, and peer review your manuscript. They will only publish quality work. The author pays nothing to get the book published. They will market and promote your book and help you increase your online presence and marketing potential. They make their money off royalties on book sales and licensing agreements. This is the publishing agreement and option that I have used to get both of my books published and is my recommended option for you. It requires patience and a well-written inquiry letter and book proposal.

In order to get your book published by someone else, it is typically not enough to have a quality manuscript, you *must* have a significant online presence and marketing potential. However, writing a book, and the thought process that goes along with it, is a great exercise for the mind even if it never gets published. You could also self-publish and use the books as promotional resources for your clients.

Chapter 12: Create and Cultivate Your Brand

Recommended Activities

1. Find your identity. What do you want to be known for professionally?
2. Identify your area of specialty.
3. Become an expert utilizing the techniques described herein.
4. Create credentials for yourself utilizing the techniques described herein.
5. Become a mentor to a young aspiring entrepreneur.
6. Build your identity by growing your brand in your area of specialty.
7. Seek recognition by joining associations related to your area of practice and applying for consideration.
8. Share your work with your industry, your peers, and your community by getting published or making presentations.
9. Write a book, even if you have to self-publish or not publish it at all. The experience of putting your thoughts on paper will be useful practice, and the forced and regulated thinking can result in original thoughts.

CHAPTER 13

Give Back

*True fulfillment comes to those who do good with-
out expecting anything in return.*

This chapter will focus on giving back to the community and to your profession by sharing knowledge and imparting wisdom. Many of the suggested avenues to give back, mentioned in this chapter, are the same as those from the previous chapter on create and cultivate your brand. However, I will touch on them again to demonstrate and emphasize how executing the same task can have multiple benefits. They can serve to create a name for yourself as well as serve to give back to your community and to your profession. That will be our focus in this chapter: How to use the same avenues of Chapter 12, as well as others, to give back to your community and to your profession.

Giving back includes imparting specialized knowledge, advice, and support to your community as well as to students and young professionals in your chosen field. It can be extremely rewarding and fulfilling to help provide valuable and useful information or service to your community or to help a young person achieve their professional goals. Chances are good that if you are successful, you got help along the way from others. It is only fair to pay it forward and help others on their way up. One of the benefits of giving back, in this form, is the passing along of knowledge, creating a legacy of ideas, principles and methods, that would normally not be passed along. Whether it be knowledge that you have gained from personal experience or passing along knowledge that you have obtained from others, it is equally beneficial. It also can be greatly beneficial to get your name out there as someone willing to take the time to share what they have learned with others.

This is not to minimize or discount giving to the less fortunate or providing counsel to those in need. That is a noble cause that should be pursued by all with the means to do so. You will find that the older you get, the closer to judgment day, the more this form of giving fills a need. Philanthropic giving is the giving of material goods or time to help the less fortunate. The cost is time and treasure. The benefit is intangible. To give back philanthropically requires selflessness, social responsibility, and the desire to change lives. You should give in this form without expecting anything in return. I believe that the true measure of a person is how they have influenced and affected, in a positive way, those they leave behind.

All forms of giving have a cost (expense) and a benefit (income) associated with them. Giving back to the community, and to your profession, involves the sharing of your knowledge, and the giving of your time, to help make a difference. Whether it be helping the community or our youth. The cost is time. The benefits are many and include publicity, name recognition, job origination, expert designation, increased networking opportunities, and credibility. To give back to your community and to your profession requires experience, knowledge, and the desire to affect change.

I have identified eight forms of giving back to the community and to your profession that I have found most beneficial and most rewarding in my career. I have included my personal experiences in each and how I came about the opportunity in the hopes that I will inspire you to potentially do the same. They are the following:

1. *Writing a book*: The best way to give back and share your knowledge with your community and your profession is to write a book. By writing a book, you not only impart knowledge to the most people, you also create a knowledge legacy that can educate and inspire people well into the future. If you are successful and are considered an expert in your field, there should be no shortage of topics you can think of to share. This is one of the hardest options to choose from, as a form to give back, due to the time commitment required. Many successful people will talk about it, but very few will do it. I recall one of my bosses talking about it all the time. Sadly, he never got the chance. If I can write a book, certainly you can too if you put forth the effort. In my case, it has been one of the most rewarding accomplishments in my career. I never thought I would, or could,

ever become a published author. Yet, I set my mind on it, laid out my goals, planned it out, prepared, and the end result was my first book titled *Engineer to Entrepreneur: Success Strategies to Manage You Career and Start Your Own Firm* published by the American Society of Civil Engineers (ASCE). The way it developed, once I decided to write it, was through my association with ASCE, having been a member of the ASCE Architectural Engineering Institutes (AEI) curtain wall committee, and being asked to prepare a webinar that would be sponsored by the committee. That opportunity allowed me to create a rapport with the publication and media branch of ASCE and opened the doors for our future collaboration. The impetus for writing the book was as a result of being asked to speak about my experiences of opening my own engineering firm by a professional engineering association. Members of which I met at a networking event for my college of engineering alumni association. Needless to say that I went ahead with that presentation, and it was so well received that I kept being asked to present by that same organization numerous other times, as well as by many other organizations who had heard about it. The only logical outcome, in my mind, was for me to write a book. Having written the book has allowed me to meet and inspire so many people throughout the years whether during in person presentations or by allowing me to share my knowledge with so many more people that I may not ever meet. My first book was geared for engineers, and that is the audience that I targeted that book to, but the concepts of entrepreneurship stretch far beyond engineering or any single profession. That is why, I decided to write a book that would be relevant to, and inspire students and young professionals in, all professions and not just engineering. If you are interested in writing a book, you can go back to Chapter 4 (Identifying and Attaining Your Goals) and find the section where I provide an example on how to go about it. A good way to do it is by writing what is called an inquiry letter and looking up the name of the publishers that put out books in your specific topic and send them your proposal. The inquiry letter and proposal usually contains: the topic, proposed book title, a one-page introduction, the estimated number of words and pages, a completed table of contents, estimated completion date, samples of completed chapters, your bio, and answers to relevant questions such as: Who is the target audience? Why is the book unique? How many books are available in your topic? What is the market size? Why would people want or need you book?

2. *Presenting to student organizations or professional groups*: The best way to give back to your profession, and impacting an entire group of people, is to talk to them in person and look them in the eye. An alternative is to do so via video conference which is used much more prevalently due to the global pandemic of 2020. This allows you to have the most immediate and direct impact with your audience. It allows you to get a good sense of those individuals who you are profoundly affecting and who are being inspired by what you have to say. In my case, as a result of opening my own firm, networking, and the publication of my first book, I have presented to numerous student and professional organizations on both entrepreneurship and topics of interest to my profession, most of them after I became an entrepreneur. I most appreciate my experiences with those individuals who pay close attention and are impacted enough to reach out to me after the presentation or beyond, to express their gratitude. There is no better pleasure than positively affecting the lives of those you surround yourself with. A good way to do it is by reaching out to your high-school, college, or university alumni association.

3. *Mentoring*: The most effective way to impact someone, a student or young professional, in your profession is one-on-one mentoring. This allows you to impact and make a difference in the life of one person directly and vividly. In my case, I have made it a point to make myself available to any student or young professional who has a desire to succeed. Regardless if that individual is an employee, student, professional, or just an interested party. A good way to do it is by reaching out to your professional association student or young members groups.

4. *Taping a television interview, podcast, or webinar*: One of the most exciting ways to share your knowledge, with the community and your profession, is to tape a television special, podcast, or webinar. It is a great way to inform the public, in your capacity as an

expert, of potential hazards or new developments on a specific topic of interest and to help raise awareness of needed changes in your industry. In my case, I have used webinars and podcasts to caution and raise awareness directly to the public after particularly troubling natural disasters. I have also had the pleasure of being asked to tape a television special, during sweeps week, on the potential hazards to North Florida from a strong-category hurricane, especially after a very strong hurricane devastated portion of the state not too far away. The interesting part, and key to that story, is that based on the suggestion of the news anchor that I drive by an area of the city where there was much construction underway to see if I could notice anything that could prove relevant to the story; I actually did. As it turns out, I was able to identify potential defects in the installation of the windows on a very high-end condo unit on the coast. We reached out to the developer and the manufacturer of the windows of the building to inform them and comment on the findings, but received no response. Issues such as these are the ones that I see commonly in my profession, in my capacity as a consultant and special inspector, and one of the main reasons I continue to try and raise awareness of the issues in my profession. A good way to secure an interview on television is to reach out to television news editors, find out when their sweeps week is, and make a proposal. The first one is the hardest, depending on the success of the story; once you are on their radar, they will look for you in the future. A good way to participate in podcasts it to reach out to the show runners. For webinars, you can reach out to your professional organization. You can find all these individuals on LinkedIn or you can get their contact information from their company websites.

5. *Writing an article for a trade or industry magazine*: The best way to keep your profession informed of the latest trends or developments is to write a magazine article or be quoted for a story in one. It is important that you share the knowledge you have gained throughout the years to positively influence and affect your industry. This is the easiest and fastest way to get published. An article, compared to a book, is not that difficult or time consuming to write. Especially if you have the knowledge to share. In my case, I have written and con-

tributed to numerous magazine articles. In one, I was able to provide my professional opinion regarding recent changes to the building code and how it would affect the industry. In another, I was able to explain how to design safely with glass in hurricane-prone regions of the country. In many others, I was reached out to and quoted regarding my professional opinion on topics of interest that affect my industry. A good way to do it is to subscribe to your industry magazines and read some of the articles published. Look up who the authors are and make a connection. Ask them for an introduction to the editors. You can also simply find information on the editors in the front pages of the publication.

6. *Presenting a paper at a national conference*: The best way to affect your profession and your peers directly is by presenting to them in person at a professional conference. In my case, the opportunity arose while serving on a technical committee where the members were considered experts in their field and were encouraged to answer a call for papers and submit an abstract. I was able to collaborate directly with my peers and expose them to areas that they had not necessary been exposed to, such as design of exterior glazing products for hurricane-prone regions of the country. I feel that by raising awareness among my peers, there exists the potential to affect change in a positive way in how structures are designed in the future with hurricanes in mind. A good way to do it is to participate and become active in the local branch of your professional organization and subscribe to their newsletter or e-mail lists. Most professional organizations have yearly conferences and send out request for paper or abstract proposals to be presented at the conference.

7. *Speaking at a lunch and learn*: The best way to inform or update the people in your community on an issue of need or concern is to present it during breakfast or lunch. Presenting during breakfast or lunch is a great way to attract busy professionals and allow them to attend, enjoy a good meal, and get educated at the same time. In my case, when I had been asked to do so by a client, I was able to raise awareness of the need for design changes to the building codes based on investigations and observations I had made while performing hurricane damage assessments after a recent rash of hurricanes

had made landfall in the United States and the Caribbean. A good way to do it is to attend one of those events yourself and introduce yourself to the sponsoring organization representative. Present them with a well-thought-out proposal that includes the topic, the target audience, and the expected demand for such a presentation.

8. *Presenting at continuing education seminars*: The best way to give back to your profession, in a more intimate way, and get as many of them to attend your presentation is to provide continuing education credits sponsored by your local professional association. It is important to understand, for these types of presentations, that you are typically not allowed to frame the presentation as a sales pitch for yourself or your company. Remember that you are there to provide a service. If performed well, the benefits will follow. In my case, recently after I had started my own firm, I was asked to present to the Florida Structural Engineers Association (FSEA), regarding my specialty, to other engineers, after a particularly confusing transition in the code. I was able to help clarify some of the code changes and give a thorough overview of the intricacies of designing building envelope systems for hurricane mitigation. That opportunity also allowed me to make a statement as to my area of expertise after having just opened my own firm. A good way to do it is, similarly to a lunch and learn, to attend one of those events yourself and introduce yourself to the sponsoring organization representative. Present them with a well-thought-out proposal that includes the topic, the target audience, and the expected demand for such a presentation.

Chapter 13: Give Back

Recommended Activities

1. You can give back in any of the eight ways listed in the chapter; it is not my place to tell you how. However, my favorite is to mentor a student or a young professional.

CHAPTER 14

Qualities of Entrepreneurship

It is how you treat yourself and how you treat others in the practice of your profession, in such a manner that brings dignity to yourself and your profession, that is the true measure of an entrepreneur.

This chapter will focus on how you should treat others and how you should treat yourself while in the practice of your profession, in such a manner that brings dignity to yourself and your profession. There are certain things that do not get taught in school, which are the qualities necessary for all successful entrepreneurs. Being a good businessman should not be the sole measure by which a successful entrepreneur is gaged. Understanding and exemplifying these qualities in the practice of your profession is what makes you a true leader. That is not to say that you cannot be successful without these qualities, only that incorporating these qualities into your practice will not only increase your odds of success, it will also greatly increase the fulfillment aspect of the entrepreneurial journey.

These qualities can be broken down into how you should treat others, such as your clients, staff and peers (*honesty, empathy humility, clarity, and philanthropy*), understanding yourself (*self-awareness*), as well as discovering and understanding your place in and view of your professional life (*philosophy*). All of these qualities can and do manifest themselves in business and should be understood and incorporated accordingly. In this chapter, I will be providing my unique definitions of each, which may differ from the standard definition. I will also be explaining how each of these qualities, or the lack thereof, can affect your level of success.

Honesty

Being True with Others. Do not compromise your integrity, no matter the reason. You must be honest with yourself, your clients, and your staff in order to achieve fulfillment from your entrepreneurial path. If you achieve success in a dishonest manner, your subconscious will manifest negative energy in ways that you may not at first comprehend. You must be honest with your clients if you wish to cement the trust required to obtain a lengthy and mutually beneficial working relationship. You must be honest with your staff, especially during troubled times, if you wish to earn their respect, loyalty, and devotion via empathy, as opposed to resentment and suspicion through dishonesty. *Refer back to Chapter 2 (What do Entrepreneurs Think About?) and Chapter 12 (Create and Cultivate Your Brand).*

Accepting jobs, and not being able to deliver or delivering an inferior product, is a form of dishonesty, which would be a tough blow to the company's reputation. Word will get out and affect your future chances at success.

Emotional Intelligence and Empathy

Being understanding of others. To be a good and effective leader, you must understand how your clients and staff are feeling. Look at the issue from their perspective by putting yourself in their shoes. Never be dismissive of their concerns or criticisms. Always take the time to hear them out and have an open dialogue. Even if the outcome remains unchanged, a genuine display of consideration and concern will create respect between you and your clients and staff. *Refer back to Chapter 11 (Manage and Grow Your Business). Read "Emotional Intelligence" by Daniel Goleman.*

If your clients or staff feel you minimize or are dismissive of their feelings and needs, and are inflexible, that will create doubt in them of a fruitful long-term relationship with you and your company. It will not foster trust and respect. You can lose clients and staff to competitors by not taking their feeling into consideration.

Humility

Treating others with respect. The moment you believe that you have achieved success and begin treating your clients and staff differently as a result will be the exact moment and inflection point demarking the beginning of your downfall. You should always be secure in and trust the manner in which you first achieved success. Treat your small clients and staff through successful times, the same as you treated them during the lean start-up years as it relates to service, attention, and understanding. Pass the credit around to your staff and praise them for their efforts. Do not lose sight of the passion that got you where you are today. *Refer back to Chapter 12 (Create and Cultivate Your Brand).*

If your clients and staff notice a change in how you treat them because of your success, and if that treatment includes a lack of respect, you are all but guaranteed a reciprocal reaction in how they think of you and your company. That could lead to friction and an eventual parting of ways.

Clarity

Being clear with others. Great communication, or clarity in communication, can change or drive minds and opinions in your favor and help avoid misunderstandings. Being prepared with the facts and eloquently and concisely conveying a message with empathy, tact, and confidence is key in originating, or retaining, work for your company. You can be the smartest businessman of the group, but if you cannot convey your idea or message in a way that touches your audience or clients, that distinction will not effectively come across to your potential clients. Similarly, a well-written letter or e-mail can make all the difference in how a client or colleague interprets what you are trying to say. Body language and tone should also be thought of as a form of communication and are especially important so as not to give off the wrong impression or risk letting slip your true feelings in awkward situations. Such a misstep may cost you a project or client. You must be very precise and concise when you write and speak and stick to the facts. Do not clutter your letters, e-mails, or speeches with emotional or unsubstantiated information. Do not ever put anything in writing that you cannot prove or commit to. *Refer back to Chapter 11 (Manage and Grow Your Business).*

A single wrong word, look, or inflection tone can be the beginning of the downturn of a relationship, both personal and professional. If you do not practice your speeches or do not deliver them with confidence or fail to understand the material you are trying to convey to your audience, you will lose credibility. Once you lose credibility, you lose respect, and once respect is lost, the opportunities will fade, and the relationship is destined to fail.

Philanthropy

Helping others in need. Philanthropy should not only involve assisting and guiding those who are materialistically poor, it should also include assisting and guiding those who are inspirationally poor or in need of guidance. This includes advising and inspiring our youth, our community, and our profession for the common goal of improving the quality of life. It also includes being aware and taking consideration of potential injustices affecting the community where you work. Philanthropy is good business practice and should be the duty of all successful entrepreneurs. *Refer back to Chapter 13 (Give Back). Also, reread Ana VeigaMilton's piece on philanthropy in Chapter 8 (Specialize and Become an Expert).*

Giving back to the community is not only spiritually and emotionally rewarding, it fosters good will from the community and can lead to opportunities you otherwise might not receive. A business that is considered socially conscious either gains a positive public image and publicity or in turn, if not socially aware, or if perceived as indifferent to the community, it could become associated with a negative image and accrue negative publicity. You cannot run a successful company in a community without considering the social underpinnings that hold that community together. That is especially true during times of civil unrest or perceived injustices. Your opinion and action, or lack of opinion and action, in such times, can have far reaching implications on your company's success. This could be a slippery slope, so tread carefully.

Self-Awareness

Understanding Yourself. In order to know others, you must first know yourself. History is fraught with failures that occurred as a result of individuals or companies becoming involved in situations beyond their area of expertise either due to a misguided drive to succeed or pressure from outside. You must get to know and understand your professional as well as your personal limitations. To do that, you must get to know yourself intimately. You must identify your strengths and weakness, your likes and dislikes, and what makes you happy. I recommend you perform an honest self-evaluation and self-interview. First, purchase a unique-looking journal that stands out. Write down the interview questions (recommended list given next) on a separate page and write your answers down beneath each question and date the answers. The questions may seem similar, but they are phrased in such a way as to get you to see yourself from different perspectives. Feel free to go back and change your answers based on how you answer each question. When you are comfortable with all your answers, reflect on yourself and see if there is something missing and if there is something you would like to work on. Then, come back to your journal periodically and compare your answers. I suspect that later in life, you will see your answers changing, as you mature and change with time. The questions I suggest asking yourself include:

1. What have been your most enjoyable moments in life, to date? Reflect on the times of greatest joys, memorable events that are engrained in your psyche that bring a smile to your face. Note who you were with during those moments and what year they occurred as well as why it was significant to you.

2. What do you love? Focus on the concepts and intangible ideas that bring joy and a smile to your face.

3. What do you enjoy doing? Focus on tangible activities that bring joy to your life. Things that you look forward to doing, eating, visiting, discussing.

4. What do you believe in? Focus on the concepts and intangible ideas that you know to be true.

5. What are your core beliefs? Focus on the concepts, ideas, and qualities that you feel strongest about and will not compromise on.

6. What does it take to make you happy? Happiness and success go hand in hand. Refer back to Chapter 4 (Identify and Attain Your Goals). Everyone has a unique definition of happiness, and that should go hand in hand with questions 7, 8, and 9 to follow. Your definition of happiness should correlate with your definition of success and should be related to the goals you set for yourself in life. What is your unique and personal definition of happiness?

7. What is your definition of success? Take your unique definition of happiness and find a vocation or profession or lifestyle and mindset that helps you best achieve happiness or best affords you the opportunity to achieve happiness. What is your unique and personal definition of success?

8. What are your goals in life? Take your unique definition of success and set small attainable subgoals that best helps you achieve success. List those goals.

9. What do you want to accomplish in the next 1, 5, or 10 years? Take those smaller subgoals and put an attainable timeframe to achieve them and make sure to take positive steps to attain them each month.

10. What are your biggest fears? What are you most afraid of? What prevents you from being happy, achieving success, or attaining your goals?

Refer back to Chapter 4 (Identify and Attain Your Goals), Chapter 5 (Do Not Be Afraid to Take Risks), and Chapter 9 (Do Not Be Afraid to Fail) to assist in answering the preceding questions. If you put forth a sincere effort in answering these questions, you will get to know the real you and only then can you really get to know others and identify what makes you happy. From there, it should be much easier to identify your ultimate goal and your unique definition of success.

You must truly understand yourself, including your own limitations, strengths, and weaknesses, in order to be a good leader. Taking risks without being informed, or compromising integrity just to secure a job, are not risks worth taking. A good leader will not bite off more than they can chew and will never be afraid to ask for help or say no. Putting yourself, or your clients and staff, in physical or financial danger in order to achieve success can lead to harm, financial ruin, or worse.

Philosophy

Understanding Your Place in Life. In order to effectively set goals and achieve success, you need to understand your core values and beliefs. You must discover and understand how far you are willing to go and sacrifice to achieve success. You need to identify your philosophy of life. Most people live by no philosophy, instead they default into accumulating material property as a sign of success. They have adopted the philosophy of "keeping up with the Jones's" and will spend more than they make on a yearly basis without consideration of the consequences.

The very fact that you have chosen to be, or are considering being, an entrepreneur, means that you are willing to think differently than most people. You want to take the road less traveled, or, even bolder, you want to choose and create your own path. The entrepreneurial philosophy entails constant learning and keeping an open mind, not being afraid of taking educated and informed risks and being an investor and not a mindless consumer. *Refer back to Chapter 1 (What is an Entrepreneur?), Chapter 2 (What do Entrepreneurs Think About?), Chapter 3 (What is Entrepreneurial Mindset?), Chapter 6 (Focus on Investing, Not on Consuming), and Chapter 7 (Accumulate Assets, Not Liabilities). Read "Rich Dad, Poor Dad" by Robert Kiyosaki.*

An entrepreneur's philosophy is centered around success, which, if they defined honestly, will also lead to happiness. However, if not truly defined, or if defined dishonestly, may lead to fame and financial wealth, but never truly to success. History recounts of many individuals who had much fame, success, and wealth that were not happy. The phrase "money cannot buy happiness" is a testament to many individuals following the wrong path to success. Therefore, if I can leave you with one final piece of advice, it is to "To thine own self be true." Take the time to discover what makes you happy and base your goals on that. This is the path to success.

Chapter 14: Qualities of Entrepreneurship

Recommended Activities

1. Look at the sections in italic at the end of each of the seven qualities and skim those chapters and sections to refresh them in your mind.
2. Perform the self-interview recommended in the section on self-awareness.
3. Take positive steps to ensure your definitions of happiness and success are symbiotic and true to yourself.
4. Read *Emotional Intelligence* by Daniel Goleman.
5. Read *Rich Dad, Poor Dad* by Robert Kiyosaki.

Closing Statement

Entrepreneurship is not an easy path to take, in fact, it can be an exceedingly difficult and trying experience at times. There will be good times, and there will be bad times. You will experience success as well as failure along the way. You will question, at times, why you did it, as well as count your blessings for having done it. It takes a person with fortitude, patience, and resilience to embark on the entrepreneurial path. However, if you have those qualities, or if you manage to get past the hurdles that come with owning your own business, despite not having those qualities, it can be an extremely rewarding and liberating path and experience. I highly recommend you take the risk, but I would caution you to do so only after much thought, preparation, and planning.

Whereas following the advice presented in this book will not guarantee success, it will provide information that will ensure the highest level of preparedness that is required to embark on the entrepreneurial path. Entrepreneurship is not for everyone, so if you feel inspired to take that leap, it is the author's sincere desire that after having read this book, you feel you will be taking that leap with many more tools and more knowledge and awareness at your disposal than before having read this book.

Starting a business is a complicated and confusing process. All that you have read in this book is the author's opinion based his experience. Please consult with an attorney, accountant, and any other qualified professional prior to starting up your own firm.

The knowledge I have shared in this book is my attempt to give back, teach, guide those who seek and thirst the knowledge that I have gained in my years. Whether I did it effectively enough is not my goal, that I did it with good intentions is the most important thing to me, and I can only hope that the lessons learned after reading this book can inspire and be of benefit to our future entrepreneurs. I would like to leave you with a final revelation...All that I have written in the preceding pages is *useless information*. That is right, it is not worth the paper it is written on. Unless, of course, you take head of what is written on these pages, which

I have shared with you based on my father's influence. I urge you to think often, act on your thoughts, put your ideas to practical use, and *tap* into your potential. Do that and you will achieve whatever goal you set out to attain.

Rick De La Guardia, B.S.A.E, E.I., M. ASCE
President and Founder of DLG Engineering, Inc.

About the Author

Rick De La Guardia is the President and Founder of DLG Engineering, Inc. (DLGE), a consulting firm specializing in the design, analysis, and forensic inspections of building envelope systems to help mitigate or assess storm damage in hurricane-prone regions of the country.

DLGE was founded in South Florida in 2009, during the height of an economic downturn, now known as the Great Recession, when many engineering firms were struggling, and opening an engineering firm was considered ill advised. A few years after its founding, DLGE was recognized by the Greater Miami Chamber of Commerce as one of the top minority-owned businesses in South Florida in 2012 and 2013. He has since gone on to found or cofound several new entrepreneurial venture companies, among them, DLG Private Ventures and Genesis Structural Engineering.

Mr. De La Guardia earned his Bachelor of Science degree in Architectural Engineering from the University of Miami in 1996. He has over 23 years of experience in designing and consulting in all aspects of the glazing field, including inspection, peer review, forensic investigation, expert witness investigations, and product testing and certification.

He is the author of a book on engineering entrepreneurship titled *Engineer to Entrepreneur: Success Strategies to Manage Your Career and Start Your Own Firm* published by the American Society of Civil Engineers (ASCE Press) that is consistently ranked in the top 100 on Amazon's bestsellers ranking for civil engineering books. He has presented to numerous student and professional engineering associations on entrepreneurship, leadership, and success.

In addition to promoting entrepreneurship, Mr. De La Guardia has presented and written on other topics such as "Hazard Mitigation Design of the Building Envelope" (Florida Structural Engineers Association, April 2010), "Hazard Mitigation of the Building Envelope: Are Our Building Envelopes Ready for a Powerful Storm?" (ATC-SEI Advances in Hurricane Engineering Conference, October 2012), "Hurricane Design of Glazing Systems: Understanding the Intricacies" (90-minute live webinar: American Society of Civil Engineers: January, July, and November of 2013), "Hurricane Mitigation Design of Glazing Systems: Requirements for Wind and Windborne Debris Protection" (Architectural Engineering Institute Conference, April 2013).

Mr. De La Guardia has authored numerous magazine articles, including "Allowable Strength of Glass: How to Design Safely for Today's Threats" (U.S. Glass Magazine, July 2010) and Growing Awareness: Changes in ASCE 7-10 to Affect Hurricane-Prone Regions" (Architects' Guide to Glass and Metal, December 2011).

Mr. De La Guardia served as the President of the University of Miami, College of Engineering Alumni Association, from June 2010 to May 2012, chaired an advisory committee on entrepreneurship and innovation for the University of Miami College of Engineering from March 2016 to October 2017, and was a member of the University of Miami Herbert Business School Entrepreneurship Advisory Board, representing the college of engineering, in 2017. Mr. De La Guardia is or has been a member of numerous professional organizations and technical committees, including the Florida Structural Engineers Association (FSEA), Latin Builders Association (LBA), and the American Society of Civil Engineers (ASCE), serving on the Architectural Engineering Institute (AEI) curtain wall committee as Vice-Chair starting in 2013. He has also served as the Grand Chapter Advisor for his fraternity, Alpha Sigma Phi, Gamma Theta chapter at the University of Miami since 2017. He has a passion for entrepreneurship and helping others achieve that goal.

Index